NYONYA SPECIALTIES

THE BEST OF SINGAPORE'S RECIPES

MRS LEONG YEE SOO

TIMES EDITIONS

NYONYA SPECIALTIES THE BEST OF SINGAPORE'S RECIPES

All the recipes in this book are selected from the late Mrs Leong Yee Soo's original cookbooks, *Singaporean Cooking*, *Singaporean Cooking Vol 2*, *Celebration Cooking* and *The Best of Singapore Cooking*.

In *Singaporean Cooking* and *The Best of Singapore Cooking*, Mrs Rosa Lee, Mrs Dorothy Norris, Miss Marie Choo, Miss Patricia Lim, Mrs Dinah Sharif, Miss Iris Kng, Miss Chau Mei Po, Mrs Irene Oei and Miss Monica Funk were acknowledged for their help in making those books possible.

For this new book, the Publisher wishes to thank **Ms Sandra Sunderiage of Arnap International**, **Mr Keng of Tong Mern Sern Anquiques Arts & Crafts**, **Singapore Museum Shop by Banyan Tree** and **Mdm Hatijah Mohd Hassan** for the loan of their crockery and utensils, and cooking and baking equipment; **Mdm Hamidah Omar**, **Mr Edmond Ho** and **Mrs Laurie Wiluan** for the use of their beautiful batik sarongs and materials.

Managing Editor : Jamilah Mohd Hassan
Editor : Sim Ee Waun
Art Direction/Designer : Christopher Wong
Photographer : Edmond Ho
Prop Stylists : Lydia Leong, Yeo Puay Khoon and Jamilah Mohd Hassan
Food Preparation & Styling : Christopher Tan
Production Co-ordinator : Nor Sidah Haron

© 2004 Marshall Cavendish International (Asia) Private Limited

Published by Times Editions – Marshall Cavendish
An imprint of Marshall Cavendish International (Asia) Private Limited
A member of the Times Publishing Limited
Times Centre, 1 New Industrial Road, Singapore 536196
Tel: (65) 6213 9288   Fax: (65) 6285 4871   E-mail: te@tpl.com.sg
Online Bookstore: http://www.timesone.com.sg/te

Malaysian Office:
Federal Publications Sdn Berhad (General & Reference Publishing) (3024-D)
Times Subang, Lot 46, Persiaran Teknologi Subang
Subang Hi-Tech Industrial Park, Batu Tiga, 40000 Shah Alam
Selangor Darul Ehsan, Malaysia
Tel: (603) 5635 2191   Fax: (603) 5635 2706   E-mail: cchong@tpg.com.my

National Library Board Singapore Cataloguing in Publication Data

Leong, Yee Soo.
Nyonya specialties /- Leong Yee Soo. – Singapore :- Times Editions,- c2004.
p. cm. – (The best of Singapore's recipes)
Includes index.
ISBN : 981-232-648-0

1. Cookery, Peranakan. 2. Cookery, Singapore. I. Title. II. Series: The best of Singapore's recipes

TX724.5.S55
641.595957 — dc21   SLS2003034567

IPrinted in Singapore by Times Printers Pte Ltd

CONTENTS ● ● ● ● ● ●

CONTENTS

PREFACE

MY GRANDMOTHER loved to cook and she loved to cook for the family. I remember as a child licking the cake mix from the bowl and waiting anxiously for the cake to come out of the oven. Our family had the benefit of her wonderful cooking and instructions on food preparation and methodology first hand. As in the past, my grandmother would always refer to her cookbooks while cooking, and today, many of our family members still continue with the same practice.

She spent more than 20 years perfecting her skills, constantly trying to improve her skills by experimenting with new kitchen equipment, technology and recipes. She had created her own recipes to be an easy and reliable guide so that even busy working adults could prepare delicious home cooked food. Her cookbooks were very much written to serve the needs of busy families and preserve the tradition of family cooking, especially with the increasingly hectic lifestyle of Singaporeans.

In this book, the recipes have now been reproduced with a new arrangement and photographs. It continues in the same tradition of the earlier books and pays attention to the careful preparation of dishes and a good choice of ingredients. In addition, all the useful cooking tips are still included.

We hope this book gives you a chance to experience good home cooking and good memories together with family and friends, cooking and eating together.

This book is dedicated to our grandmother's memory as a great cook, a progressive woman in her field, beloved mother, grandmother and great grandmother.

LEONG PAT LYNN & LEONG SUE LYNN

CANDLENUTS

If unavailable, use almonds, cashew nuts, Brazil nuts or macadamia nuts.

COCONUT

The milk from the coconut you use plays a very important part in the type of food or cakes that you are preparing. Be very careful and selective when choosing a coconut.

Coconuts do not come in one standard size, age and richness.

- The skinned, grated coconut referred to throughout the book is coconut which has the brown skin removed. This is to give the milk an extra whiteness. It also gives a rich natural colour to the food.
- When buying a coconut, bear in mind the type of food or cake you are preparing. For most types of food that require coconut milk, choose a freshly cut coconut with a dark brown skin as this gives rich and sweet milk. For cakes, you need to see to the requirements of your recipe. For example, if the recipe calls for 'coarsely grated coconut' then you should choose one that has a light brown skin; it is younger than the dark brown and is tender and not stringy. For special recipes like 'Sar-Sargon' you require coconut that is tender and young, ie. the skin of the coconut must be pale in colour.
- For cakes that need coarsely grated coconut to be sprinkled over, it is safer to rub a little fine salt lightly over the coconut. Place it in a shallow baking tin and steam over rapidly boiling water for 3 minutes. Cool completely before use. This will keep the coconut from turning sour.
- For every 455 g (1 lb) of grated coconut, you should be able to extract about 225–255 ml (1–1^1/8 cups) milk when the coconut is fresh. Therefore, make sure the coconut is freshly cut for the day and not one that has been cut and kept overnight. See that the coconut is free of mildew or has not turned yellow in some parts

- One interesting point to note is that the amount of milk you get from a kilogramme of grated coconut depends on the machine that grates the coconut. The rollers used in the grating machines at coconut stalls come in different degrees of fineness. As such, a machine using fine tooth rollers gives you more milk than one with coarse tooth rollers.
- To squeeze coconut for No.1 milk: take a piece of white muslin 30-cm (12-in) square, put in a small fistful, or about 55 g (2 oz), of coconut and squeeze and twist at the same time. For No.2 milk, add the amount of water required and squeeze hard.

Freezing Coconut Milk

- Buy 1.4–1.8 kg (3–4 lb) of grated coconut, squeeze for No.1 milk and set aside. Add 170 ml (^{3}/4 cup) water to each 455 g (1 lb) of coconut and squeeze for No.2 milk. Collect separately. Pour the No.1 and No.2 milk in separate ice-cube trays. When frozen, remove from ice-tray and pack into plastic bags and store in the freezer. It is very useful to have a stock of frozen coconut milk always in case you need it at any time of the day. It can be used to make curries and all types of cakes.
- To use frozen coconut milk, chop the amount required. Place a little water in a saucepan and bring to a boil. Place the frozen coconut milk in a small enamel basin, place basin over the water and allow the frozen coconut to thaw, stirring occasionally. Remove coconut milk to cool as soon as it turns liquid.

KITCHEN WISDOM & TIPS ON TECHNIQUES

Making Coconut Oil for Nyonya Cakes

In a saucepan, combine 115 g (4 oz) grated coconut, 225 ml (1 cup) corn oil and 8 screwpine (*pandan*) leaves that have been cut into pieces. Bring to a boil and cook until coconut turns dark brown. Pour oil through a metal sieve and cool before use. Store in refrigerator to preserve freshness and for future use.

COOKING MEAT

Pork chops should be cooked over moderate heat in a very hot pan or grilled under a hot grill. This will seal in the meat juices. Brown on both sides, turning over twice; then turn it down to medium heat and cook until done, about 15–20 minutes.

For bacon, cut off the rind and snip the fat in two or three places to prevent bacon from curling during frying.

Fillet steak is the best and most tender of meat cuts; next comes sirloin, scotch, porterhouse, rump and minute steak. Marinating a steak before cooking not only gives it a better flavour but also helps to make it tender. Minute steak, however, is best grilled or fried without marinating.

COOKING OIL AND FATS

To get the best results, particularly when cooking Chinese dishes, use an equal portion of both lard and cooking oil. It gives the dish a special fragrance. In recipes that specifies that lard is preferable to cooking oil, use lard in order to get its distinct flavour.

For deep-frying, always use either refined deodorised coconut oil, palm cooking oil or corn oil. Do not use olive oil.

COOKING VEGETABLES

To fry leafy vegetables, separate the leaves from the stalk. The stalks should be placed in the pan together with any other ingredients and cooked first. Stir-fry for a minute or so before adding the leaves.

To boil and blanch vegetables, bring a saucepan of water to the boil over very high heat. When the water is boiling, add some salt, sugar and a tablespoonful of cooking oil. Add the stalks, cook for $1/2$ minute and then add the leaves. Cook for another $1/2$ minute. Use a wire ladle to remove the vegetables and drain in a colander. Rinse under a running tap and drain well before use.

Vegetables like long beans and cabbage should be cooked for 5–7 minutes only, to retain their sweetness and crispness.

When boiling bean sprouts it is important to place them in boiling water for 1 minute. Do not add any cooking oil. Remove and drain with a wire ladle. Transfer to a basin of cold water and soak for 10 minutes or until cold. Spread thinly in a colander until ready for use. The bean sprouts will then keep without 'souring'.

FRYING

1. Before frying, ensure that the the pan is very hot before you pour in the cooking oil. To get the best results when frying vegetables:
   - Use an iron wok (*kuali*) as it can take and retain extreme heat, which is most important.
   - Add the cooking oil to a smoking hot wok. This prevents food from sticking to the bottom. But do not allow the oil to become smoking hot as overheated fat or oil turns bitter and loses its fine flavour.
2. For deep-frying, the cooking oil must be smoky, that is, when a faint haze of smoke rises from the oil. It is then ready for frying.
   - When deep-frying in large quantities, put enough food in the pan and keep the oil boiling all the time.

- Make sure the fat is heated until smoking hot each time you put in food to be fried.
- When frying large pieces of meat or a whole chicken, the heat must be very high for the first 5 minutes to seal in the juices. After that, lower the heat for the rest of the cooking time. This gives the meat or chicken a nice golden colour and allows it to be cooked right through.

3. After frying food that is coated with flour or breadcrumbs (this also seals in the meat juices), filter the oil through a wire sieve lined thinly with cotton wool. The oil will come out clean and free from sediments.
   - Add more fresh oil to the strained oil for future use.
4. Cooking oil that has been used to deep-fry fish and prawns should be kept separate for future use and kept for cooking fish and prawns only.
5. You may clarify hot oil by squeezing some lemon juice into it, but remember to turn off the heat first. Strain and store for future use.
6. Butter will not take intense heat when frying, so put in some cooking oil before the butter.
7. Dust food with seasoned flour before coating with or dipping in batter for frying.

KAFFIR LIME LEAVES

Locally called *daun limau purut*, it has waxy dark green, double leaves with a distinct fragrance. To slice finely, roll it up tightly and slice thinly parallel to the central vein. Discard the central vein which will come out in one complete strip after slicing.

LARD

The oil extracted from pork fat after it has been fried is called lard. Dice the pork fat before frying. Do not overcook or burn the fat, otherwise the oil extracted will be dark and bitter. Unlike butter or margarine, lard can take intense heat without burning so it is most suitable for food that has to be cooked over high heat.

LEMON GRASS

Lemon grass gives a pleasant fragrance to cooked dishes. Use lemon rind as a substitute only when this is not available. The fragrance comes from the bottom 7 cm (3 in) of the stalk nearest the root end. The green outer layer is removed before use. To bruise or crush lemon grass, bash with the flat surface of a cleaver or chopper.

LIME PASTE

The lime paste mentioned in some of the recipes refers to the white chalky edible lime that is used for betelnut chewing. It can be bought at any Indian grocer.

Chillies retain their crispness in certain recipes when they are soaked in lime water.

SEASONING

The salt used in many of these recipes is local fine salt and not the fine table salt. Fine table salt is used mostly in Western cakes where it can be sifted together with the flour. As table salt is finer, it is more salty than the local fine salt. So measure less salt if you use fine table salt.

Use your discretion when seasoning with salt, sugar, chilli or tamarind pulp (*asam*). Season to your own taste as there is no hard and fast rule for seasoning food. However, for cakes, one must be precise and follow the recipe to get the best results.

MSG in recipes refers to monosodium glutamate. As a substitute, chicken stock may be used. Use 1 chicken cube for 1 tsp MSG.

KITCHEN WISDOM & TIPS ON TECHNIQUES

SCREWPINE LEAVES

Commonly called *pandan* leaves, this local plant is a rich, emerald green and has long, smooth pointed leaves. It imparts a special fragrance and is used widely in Asian desserts and kuih. There is no substitute. Before tying it into a knot, tear each leaf lengthwise to release the fragrance.

SELECTING MEAT, POULTRY AND SEAFOOD

Pork

Should be pink, the fat very white and the skin thin.

Beef

Choose meat that is light red and the cross-grain smooth and fine. The same applies to mutton. Do not buy dark coloured meat with fat that is yellow.

Chicken

Fresh local chickens have a much better taste and flavour than frozen ones. Frozen chicken is more suitable for roasting, frying or grilling. When buying local chicken, select one with white, smooth skin. The tip of the breastbone should be soft and pliable when pressed with the thumb. When selecting chicken for steaming, choose one that is young and tender and weighs about 1 kg (approximately $2^1/2$ lb). For Hainanese chicken rice, choose one that is plump at the breasts and thighs and weighs 1.6–1.8 kg (approximately $3^1/2$–4 lb). For grilled chicken or roast spring chicken, choose a 680–795 g ($1^1/2$–$1^3/4$ lb) chicken. A 1.5 kg (3–$3^1/2$ lb) chicken is best for curries and other spicy dishes.

Duck

Select as for chicken. The smaller ones are mostly used for soups and the larger ducks for roasting or braising.

Fish

When buying fish, first of all make sure that the flesh is firm to the touch. The eyes should be shiny, the gills blood-red and the scales silvery white. Squeezing lemon juice over fish will whiten it and keep it firm when boiling or steaming.

Mix tamarind, salt and some sugar to marinate fish for $^1/2$ hour before cooking curries or tamarind dishes.

Prawns

Fresh prawns have shiny shells and are firm to the touch. The head is firmly attached to the body. Avoid buying prawns with heads loosely hanging on.

Cuttlefish

When cuttlefish is very fresh, the body is well rounded, firm and shiny. The head is stuck fast to the body and the ink pouch in the stomach is firmly attached.

SUBSTITUTE INGREDIENTS

- The purplish variety of onion is a good substitute for shallots.
- If fresh ginger, lemon grass and galangal are not easily available, use the powdered forms.
- It is always advisable to use powdered turmeric.
- Almonds, cashew nuts, Brazil nuts or macadamia nuts can be used if candlenuts are not available.

THICKENING

For Chinese dishes, thickening means to thicken the gravy so as to coat the food rather than have the gravy running over the serving plate. Cornflour is a common thickening agent and refers to tapioca flour sold in the local markets. It is also known as sago flour (refined quality, and not the type used to starch clothes).

ALUMINIUM FRYING PANS

Suitable for deep-frying as they retain a steady heat and give food a nice golden brown colour. Frying chilli paste in an aluminium pan will give the mixture a natural bright colour whereas an iron wok (*kuali*) will result in a darker paste, possibly with a slight taste of iron.

ALUMINIUM SAUCEPAN

The heavy flat-bottomed pan is the best buy. It is suitable for the electric or gas stove. Food is cooked easily without burning. A thin saucepan will buckle when it is overheated and will not be in contact with the electric hot plate.

CHINA CLAYPOT

Chicken and pork are usually braised and stewed in the China claypot. It simmers food very nicely without burning and has a lower rate of evaporation than other saucepans. It also retains the special flavour of foods and is widely used in Chinese homes. It is also used to cook rice and porridge. Buy one with a smooth, glazed finish.

COPPER PANS

Copper pans are rarely used for Asian recipes. A copper pan has its own rare qualities. Salted mustard has a very bright green colour when boiled in a copper pan. Copper pans are very rarely used, however, as they are very expensive.

ENAMEL SAUCEPAN

Enamel saucepans are more suitable for soups and certain types of food that contain acid like tamarind or vinegar. Chipped enamelware is vulnerable to rust.

IRON WOK

Most Chinese prefer the iron wok (*kuali*) to the aluminium one chiefly because the iron wok can retain extreme heat before the other ingredients are added. In an iron wok, food cooks in a shorter period of time and retain its flavour and crispness. The most important point to remember is that fried food and pounded ingredients will not stick to the bottom of the wok when it is well heated.

To season an iron wok

Place some grated coconut and water until it fills up three-quarters of the wok, and boil until dry. Stir occasionally until the coconut turns black, approximately 3–4 hours.

Daily care: Do not use any detergent. Wipe wok well after each wash. If it is to be stored for a long period, grease wok lightly to prevent rust.

NON-STICK PANS

There are many brands of non-stick pans to select from. Choose carefully. Whenever possible, buy the best quality products as they work out to be the most cost effective in the long run.

Some points to remember when using non-stick pans

- Non-stick pans are ideal for frying fish and soft bean curd. In a non-stick pan, food that is to be braised or simmered require less liquid. Food does not burn easily in a non-stick pan nor does the gravy evaporate as quickly as in an ordinary pan.
- The Teflon in a non-stick pan should not be heated through. If this happens, the pan may lose its non-stick qualities. Since stir-frying requires high heat, do not stir-fry in a non-stick pan. It is always best to stir-fry in an iron wok.
- Do not use the non-stick pan as a steamer as it will again damage the Teflon.
- Never use a metal slice on a non-stick pan.
- Always pour in the cooking oil or gravy first before putting on the heat.

KITCHEN EQUIPMENT

PESTLE AND MORTAR
Insist on local granite which is white with black/grey spots. To season the pounder, grind a small handful of fine sea sand in the mortar until both the pestle and mortar are reasonably smooth.

STAINLESS STEEL PANS
Stainless steel pans look attractive and are easily cleaned, but do not heat evenly. Food burns easily, too.

SUPPLEMENTARY RECIPES

Crisp-fried Shallots
Many recipes call for crisp-fried shallots to be used as a flavourful garnish.

- Peel and slice shallots thinly and dip in salt water for a while. Rinse and drain well.
- Scatter sliced shallots on absorbent paper to dry or roll up in a tea towel for $1/2$ hour. Heat enough cooking oil for deep-frying until smoking hot. Add the sliced shallots and stir-fry over high heat until shallots turn light brown.
- Reduce the heat and continue stirring until the shallots are light golden brown. Remove at once with a wire sieve to drain. Scatter on absorbent paper to cool.
- Store in a clean, dry bottle immediately. The shallots keep crisp for months in an airtight bottle.

Fried Pounded Garlic

- Peel and pound garlic or use blender to mince the garlic.
- Place garlic in a wire sieve and immerse in salt water. Drain. Use a thin piece of muslin to further squeeze out the water.
- In a heated wok, add enough cooking oil for deep-frying. When the oil is smoking hot, put the garlic and stir-fry until it turns light brown. Reduce the heat to very low and continue stirring until garlic becomes a light golden brown.
- Remove at once with a wire sieve and scatter on absorbent paper. Cool and store as for crispy shallots.

Note:
The crispy shallots and garlic do not retain much oil when the heat is turned up just before removing from wok.

Rice

- Wash rice until water runs clear.
- Use 55 ml (¹/₄ cup) of water for every 30 g (1 oz) of rice.
- For 455 g (16 oz) of rice, use between 800–910 ml (3¹/₂–4 cups) water, depending on the quality of the rice.
- Boil the rice until the water evaporates, leaving steam holes when dry. Reduce heat to low and cook for a further ¹/₂ hour. About 455 g (1 lb) of rice is sufficient for 8 servings.

Dried Chilli Paste

Dried chillies	225 g (8 oz), stems removed
Water	450 ml (2 cups)

- Place chillies in a saucepan three-quarter filled with cold water.
- Bring to a boil and cook for 5 minutes. Cover pan and leave chillies to soak for 10 minutes. Drain.
- Place chillies in a large basin and wash until water runs clear. Drain.
- Using an electric blender, blend half of the chillies with 225 ml (1 cup) water until very fine. Remove paste and repeat process with the other half of the chillies and water.
- Store chilli paste in a plastic container. Keep in freezer until needed.

Note:
Keep chilli paste rotating while blending. Add a little water if paste is stuck.

This recipe makes about 32 Tbsp of chilli paste.

Wet Rice or Glutinous Rice Flour

Fine rice or glutinous rice flour	625g (22 oz)
Cold water	425 ml (1³/₄ cups and 2 Tbsp)

- Place flour in a mixing bowl and gradually pour in the cold water. Stir until it becomes a firm paste.
- Use the amount required for each recipe and keep the remainder in the freezer for future use.

Note:
- The paste will keep in the freezer for 1–2 months if stored in plastic bags flattened to 2.5 cm (1 inch) thick slabs.
- Recommended brands: Superior Quality Thai Rice and Glutinous Rice Flour (Erawan Brand); Fine Rice Flour (Seagull trademark); freshly ground wet rice or glutinous rice flour are available at local wet markets.

Alkaline Water

White alkaline crystal	625 g (22 oz)
Hot water	680 ml (3 cups)

- Place alkaline crystal in a porcelain jar or bowl. Add the hot water and stir with a wooden spoon to dissolve the crystals. Let it stand overnight.
- Strain alkaline water through a fine muslin. Store the alkaline water in a bottle for future use.

Note:
- Prepared alkaline water can be kept for almost a year. Store in a bottle.
- Alkaline water is now available at specialty bakery suppliers such as Phoon Huat.

appetisers&nibbles

NYONYA SPECIALTIES – THE BEST OF SINGAPORE'S RECIPES

Ngoh Hiang

MEAT ROLLS

INGREDIENTS

Dried bean curd skin	2 pieces
Eggs	2, lightly beaten
Pork	455 g (1 lb), minced
Prawns	225 g (8 oz), shelled, deveined and coarsely chopped
Onion	1, peeled and finely chopped
Crab meat	170 g (6 oz), steamed
Cooking oil for deep-frying	
Cucumber	$^{1}/_{2}$, sliced for garnishing

Seasoning

Salt	1 tsp
Sugar	2 tsp
MSG	1 tsp, optional
Soy sauce	2 tsp
Dark soy sauce	1 tsp
Pepper	1 tsp
Lard or cooking oil	1 Tbsp
Plain flour	1 Tbsp
Five-spice powder	1 rounded tsp

METHOD

- Cut bean curd skin into rectangles 15 cm x 18 cm (6 in x 7 in). Set aside.
- Prepare the filling: In a large bowl, combine seasoning ingredients with the eggs, then add pork, prawns, onion and the crab meat. Mix well.
- Place a small portion of the filling mixture on a piece of bean curd skin and roll into a cigar shape. Seal ends with a little plain flour mixed with water.
- Steam the *ngoh hiang* for 10 minutes, then leave to cool.
- Now, deep-fry them.
- When cool, slice and serve with cucumber.

Otak–Otak Panggang

SPICY FISH GRILLED IN BANANA LEAVES

INGREDIENTS

Coconut	680 g (1¹/₂ lb), grated
Spanish mackerel (*ikan tenggiri*)	1.2 kg (2 lb 11 oz)
Water	170 ml (³/₄ cup)
Salt	A pinch
Eggs	2, lightly beaten
Kaffir lime leaves (*daun limau purut*)	2, finely sliced
Turmeric leaves (*daun kunyit*)	4, finely sliced
Banana leaves	26, cut into 22 cm x 20 cm (10 in x 8 in) sheets, washed and scalded

Rempah

Onions	2, about 225 g (8 oz), peeled
Galangal	30 slices, about 85 g (3 oz), peeled
Candlenuts	5, crushed
Dried chillies	25, soaked to soften
Shrimp paste (*belacan*)	1 Tbsp
Turmeric	20 g, peeled

Seasoning

Sugar	3 Tbsp
Salt	2 Tbsp
MSG	1 tsp, optional
Cooking oil	3 Tbsp
Coriander seeds	2 tsp, roasted

METHOD

- Using a piece of muslin, squeeze grated coconut to extract 285 ml (1¹/₄ cups) of No. 1 milk. Collect in a bowl and set aside.
- Combine *rempah* ingredients and grind to a fine paste. Set aside.
- Bone and fillet the fish. Using a spoon, scrape half of the meat into a bowl. Thinly slice the remaining meat.
- Pound or mince the scraped fish meat until smooth. Add 170 ml (³/₄ cup) water and a pinch of salt. Beat mixture with your hands until it forms a sticky paste.
- Add the No. 1 milk and continue beating until well blended. Add the eggs, *rempah* paste and seasoning ingredients and mix thoroughly until well blended. Add the sliced fish, lime leaves and turmeric leaves and mix well.
- Place 2 Tbsp of fish mixture in the middle of each banana leaf, fold it into a long rectangular package and fasten the two ends of the leaf with a stapler or a sharp toothpick.
- Preheat grill. When very hot, place wrapped fish about 8 cm (3 in) from the hot grill, and cook for 7−10 minutes on each side.

Poh Pia

FRESH SPRING ROLLS

INGREDIENTS

Poh pia skin (ready-to-use)	625 g (1 lb 6 oz)

Filling

Streaky pork	900 g (2 lb)
Salt	A pinch
Prawns	455 g (1 lb), small
Cooking oil	225 ml (1 cup)
Garlic	8 Tbsp, peeled and pounded (about 30 cloves)
Yellow bean paste (*taucheo*)	8 Tbsp, pounded
Salt	1–1¹/₂ Tbsp
Sugar	8 Tbsp
MSG	2 tsp, optional
Jicama (*bangkuang* or yam bean)	1.8 kg (4 lb), peeled and shredded
Bamboo shoots	800 g (4 lb), boiled tender and shredded
Firm bean curd (*taukwa*)	12 pieces, cut into thin strips and fried

Topping

Cucumber	900 g (2 lb), skinned, seeded and finely shredded
Bean sprouts	900 g (2 lb), picked, washed and scalded
Chinese parsley (coriander leaves)	8 sprigs, washed and drained
Local lettuce	455 g (1 lb), washed and drained
Crab meat	225 g (8 oz), steamed
Prawns	455 g (1 lb), shelled and deveined, fried and sliced lengthwise
Eggs	8, lightly beaten, fried into an omelette and thinly sliced
Chinese sausages	4, fried and thinly sliced
Sweet black sauce (*kicap pekat manis*)	280 ml (1¹/₄ cups)

INGREDIENTS

Garlic	30 cloves, peeled and pounded to a fine paste
Garlic	30 cloves, peeled and pounded and fried until crisp
Red chillies	455 g (1 lb), pounded to a fine paste

METHOD

To cook filling

- In a saucepan, combine pork, a pinch of salt and 1 litre (4¹/₂ cups) water and bring to the boil for 45 minutes. Remove pork and slice into fine strips. Set aside 455 ml (2 cups) of the stock.
- Shell and devein prawns. Pound prawn shells and add 1 litre (4¹/₂ cups) water. Strain and set aside the stock.
- Heat cooking oil in a wok and fry pounded garlic until light brown. Add yellow bean paste, salt, sugar and MSG, if using. Stir-fry for 1 minute. Pour in the prawn stock and bring to a boil.
- Add jicama to cook, then add bamboo shoots and the 455 ml (2 cups) pork stock. Boil for ¹/₂ hour over moderate heat.
- Lower heat, add fried bean curd strips and sliced pork. Cook for 1¹/₂ hours, stirring occasionally.
- Add the prawns and cook for a further 10 minutes.
- Transfer filling to a saucepan. Simmer until ready to serve.

To serve *poh pia*

- Place cucumber, bean sprouts, Chinese parsley, lettuce, crab meat, prawns, egg omelette and sausages on separate serving plates.
- Place the sweet black sauce, garlic paste, fried garlic and chilli paste in separate bowls.
- Arrange the *poh pia* skins and the egg skins, if using, on separate plates.
- Place the filling in a large deep bowl.

Note:
Keep *Poh Pia* skin covered with a damp cloth until ready to use. As a variation, you can also make your own egg skin (*recipe on page 21*).

To assemble *poh pia*

- Place a skin on a plate and spread the topping in this order: a little sweet black sauce, garlic paste and chilli paste.
- Add a piece of lettuce, some bean sprouts, shredded cucumber and a heaped spoonful of filling.
- Top with some Chinese sausages, egg omelette, prawns and crab meat. Sprinkle over with some Chinese parsley and crispy garlic and fold into a neat roll.
- Cut and serve.

Egg Poh Pia Skin

INGREDIENTS

Plain flour	285 g (10 oz)
Cornflour	3 Tbsp
Salt	A pinch
Eggs	10
Water	680–740 m (3–3¹⁄₄ cups)
Cooking oil	85 ml (¹⁄₃ cup)

METHOD

- Combine plain flour, cornflour, salt and sieve into a mixing bowl.
- In another bowl, beat eggs lightly, then add water and cooking oil.
- Add egg mixture to the flour and mix to form a batter.
- Grease a well-heated omelette pan. Pour enough batter to form a thin layer over the base of the pan, like a pancake. Cook until the edges curl slightly.
- Tranfer the skin onto a plate. Repeat process until all the batter is used up.

Kuih Pie Tee

SHREDDED BAMBOO SHOOTS IN PATTY CASES

INGREDIENTS

Patty Cases

Egg	1, large, lightly beaten
Water	225 ml (1 cup)
Salt	A pinch
Plain flour	115 g (4 oz), sifted
Cooking oil for deep-frying	

Filling

Streaky pork	455 g (1 lb)
Water	680 ml (3 cups)
Salt	A pinch
Small prawns	225g (8 oz), shelled and deveined (keep shells)
Lard or cooking oil	4 Tbsp
Garlic	2 Tbsp, peeled and pounded
Bamboo shoots	1.2 kg (2 lb 11 oz), boiled tender, and finely shredded
Jicama (*bangkuang* or yam bean)	300 g (11 oz), peeled and finely shredded
Firm bean curd (*taukwa*)	2 large pieces, cut into thin strips and fried

Seasoning

Salt	1/2 tsp
MSG	1/2 tsp, optional
Sugar	2 Tbsp
Yellow bean paste (*taucheo*)	2 Tbsp, pounded

Topping

Crab meat	225 g (8 oz), steamed
Prawns	225g (8 oz), shelled and fried with a pinch of salt and finely diced
Chinese parsley (coriander leaves)	3 sprigs
Garlic	4 Tbsp, pounded and fried crisp
Eggs	2, fried into thin omelettes and shredded

METHOD

To prepare patty cases

- Combine egg, water and salt in a bowl.
- Pour mixture gradually into the flour and mix to form a smooth batter.
- Sieve into a bowl and leave to stand for 1/2 hour.
- In a wok, heat cooking oil for deep-frying. Dip the *kuih pie tee* mould (*see inset picture*) in the hot oil and heat for 2 minutes.
- Now dip the mould into the batter and return it to the hot oil and deep-fry until batter is light brown and retains its shape when it slips away from the mould.
- Place patty cases on absorbent paper. Cool and store in an airtight container to retain crispness.

To cook filling

- Cook pork in 455 ml (2 cups) water and a pinch of salt for 1/2 hour. Remove and cut into fine strips. Set aside. Retain the stock as well for use later.
- Pound prawn shells. Add the remaining 225ml (1 cup) water and mix well. Strain and set aside prawn stock.
- Heat lard or cooking oil in a wok. Fry pounded garlic until brown, then add seasoning ingredients. Stir-fry for 1/2 minute.
- Add bamboo shoots and jicama, prawn stock and pork stock. Cook for 45 minutes over moderate heat.
- Add prawns, pork and bean curd strips. Stir and cook until almost dry.
- Transfer to a large plate to cool before using.

To serve

- Place filling in a large bowl.
- Place topping ingredients in separate bowls.
- Fill patty cases with filling and sprinkle over with a variety of topping. Serve with chilli sauce.

Note:
Dip shredded jicama in cold water to remove the starch. Drain it before cooking.

Kuih Chang Babi

GLUTINOUS RICE DUMPLING WITH PORK FILLING

INGREDIENTS

Rice

Glutinous rice	2 kg (4^1/$_2$ lb), soaked overnight
Salt	3 Tbsp
Pepper	3 tsp
Water	510 ml (2^1/$_4$ cups)
Lard	420 g (15 oz)
Screwpine (*pandan*) leaves	30–35, large, about 8 cm x 55 cm (3^1/$_2$ in x 22 in)

Filling

Water	850 ml (3^3/$_4$ cups)
Lean pork	1.2 kg (2 lb 11 oz)
Pork fat	115 g (4 oz)
Lard or cooking oil	200 ml (2 cups)
Garlic	55 g (2 oz), peeled and finely pounded
Shallots	225 g (8 oz), peeled and finely pounded
Salt	1 rounded tsp
Sugar	395 g (14 oz)
Pepper	3 Tbsp
Dark soy sauce	4 Tbsp
Dried Chinese mushrooms	55 g (2 oz), soaked and finely diced
Sugared winter melon (*tung kwa*)	225 g (8 oz), diced
Coriander seeds	6 Tbsp, roasted and ground

METHOD

To prepare rice

- Drain glutinous rice and divide into three portions.
- Using chopsticks, make steam holes in one portion of the rice. Steam over rapidly boiling water for 20 minutes.
- Remove glutinous rice and place in a saucepan.
- Combine 1 Tbsp of the salt, 1 tsp of the pepper and 170 ml (^{3}/$_4$ cup) of the water and pour around the steamed glutinous rice. Mix well.
- Cover for 10 minutes. Then mix 140 g (5 oz) of the lard evenly with the glutinous rice. Keep warm in a saucepan with a tight fitting lid.

- Repeat process with the other 2 portions of the glutinous rice.
- Put all the steamed glutinous rice in the saucepan and keep warm.

To prepare filling

- In a saucepan, combine 850 ml (3^3/$_4$ cups) water, pork and pork fat and bring to a boil. Keep it boiling over moderately high heat for 20 minutes.
- Remove pork and fat and leave aside to cool. Dice pork and fat and set aside. Continue boiling until stock is reduced to 455 ml (2 cups).
- Add lard or cooking oil to a heated wok. When hot, add the pounded garlic and pounded shallots and fry until fragrant. Add in pork, salt, sugar, pepper and dark soy sauce and stir to combine. Continue cooking until pork changes colour.
- Add the stock, mushrooms, sugared melon and pork fat and continue cooking over medium heat for ^{1}/$_2$ hour.
- Add the ground coriander and stir. Reduce heat and simmer until meat filling is almost dry. Leave to cool and keep overnight before assembling the dumplings.

To wrap dumplings

- Take 1 broad or 2 narrow screwpine leaves, fold from the centre of the leaf to form a cone. Take a fistful of steamed glutinous rice and press firmly into the cone.
- Make a well in the centre of the glutinous rice while pressing the rice evenly to the sides of the cone.
- Put 2–3 Tbsp of the pork filling in the well. Then take some of the glutinous rice which has been flattened against the sides of the cone and cover the filling.
- Fold the leaf over to cover and tie tightly with string.
- Tie dumplings in groups of 10. Boil them in a large pot of water with 2 Tbsp salt for 3–3^1/$_2$ hours.

Note:
Unwrap a dumpling to see if the rice is smooth. If not, boil for 30–40 minutes more. Hang dumplings to dry for 1–2 hours after cooking to prevent sogginess.

Sugared winter melon is available in most Chinese grocery stores.

Spicy Prawn Rolls

INGREDIENTS

Candlenuts	6
Turmeric	20 g (1 Tbsp), peeled
Shrimp paste (*belacan*)	1 tsp
Sugar	8 Tbsp
Salt	1/2 Tbsp
Tamarind pulp (*asam*)	3 Tbsp, mixed with 140 ml (1/2 cup) water, squeezed and strained
Dried prawns	340 g (12 oz), soaked and finely pounded
Cooking oil	285 ml (1 1/4 cups)
Green chillies	115 g (4 oz), thinly sliced
Red chillies	115 g (4 oz), thinly sliced
Garlic	115 g (4 oz), peeled and thinly sliced
Shallots	225 g (8 oz), peeled and thinly sliced
Lemon grass	10 stalks, sliced slantwise
Spring roll skin (ready-to-use)	50 pieces, small
Cooking oil for deep-frying	

METHOD

To prepare filling

- Pound candlenuts, turmeric and shrimp paste together to form a fine paste.
- Add sugar, salt, tamarind water and dried prawns to the spice paste, mix and set aside.
- Add cooking oil to a heated wok. When oil is hot, fry each of the sliced ingredients separately until light brown. Set aside.
- With the same oil, fry the spice mixture over low heat until almost dry. Stir constantly to prevent burning.
- Return all the fried ingredients to the wok with the spice mixture and stir-fry for another 5 minutes. Transfer to a tray and cool.
- Blend finely in an electric blender.

To make prawn rolls

- Cut the spring roll skins into quarters. Take a piece of skin and scoop 1 tsp filling onto it.
- Roll, wrap and seal the open end with a solution of plain flour and water. Repeat with the remaining skins and filling.
- In a wok, add enough cooking oil for deep-frying. When hot, deep-fry rolls over moderate heat until light brown.
- Transfer onto a kitchen towel to soak up excess oil.
- Store in an airtight container while warm.

Sambal Lengkong

CRISPY FISH GRANULES

INGREDIENTS

Coconut	1.2 kg (2 lb 11 oz), grated
Water	225 ml (1 cup)
Wolf-herring (*ikan parang*)	1.2 kg (2 lb 11 oz), washed
Salt	2 tsp
Sugar	5 Tbsp, mixed with 3 Tbsp hot water
Kaffir lime leaves (*daun limau purut*)	10

Rempah

Shallots	340 g (12 oz), peeled
Candlenuts	8, crushed
Red chillies	3, seeded
Galangal	14 slices, about 55 g (2 oz), peeled
Lemon grass	6 stalks, finely sliced

METHOD

- Combine *rempah* ingredients and pound until fine.
- Place grated coconut in a piece of muslin and squeeze to extract No.1 milk. Collect in a container. Add the 225 ml (1 cup) water to the grated coconut and squeeze again for No.2 milk. Collect in a separate container.
- Place wolf herring in a deep dish. Pour in the No.2 milk and steam over high heat until fish is cooked. Set aside.
- Remove the fish and set aside. Combine the coconut-fish stock (leftover in the dish from steaming) with the No.1 milk, *rempah* paste and salt.
- On a separate plate, debone and flake the fish very finely and return the meat to the coconut-fish stock mixture.
- Pour the fish mixture into a heated wok and fry over a moderate heat until almost dry, stirring constantly. Reduce the heat to very low and add in the sugar syrup and lime leaves. Fry until the fish granules are crispy and light brown, stirring constantly.
- Cool and store in an airtight container.

Note:
To test if the fish granules are crispy, press them between your thumb and finger. They should be grainy. Steamed fish should be mashed until fine while still hot. A mincer may also be used.

Luak Chye

MIXED VEGETABLE PICKLE IN MUSTARD DRESSING

INGREDIENTS

Young ginger	85 g (3 oz), peeled and thinly sliced
Carrot	1, skinned and thinly sliced
White radish (*daikon*)	2, skinned and thinly sliced
Salt	3 tsp
Sugar	1 Tbsp
Chinese mustard greens (*kai choy*)	455 g (1 lb), thinly sliced
French mustard	2–3 Tbsp

Pickling Mixture

Vinegar	115 ml (1/2 cup)
Water	85 ml (1/3 cup)
Sugar	4 Tbsp
Salt	3/4 tsp

METHOD

- In a bowl, combine the young ginger, carrot and white radish and season with 1 tsp salt and 1 Tbsp sugar. Set aside for 1/2 hour.
- Put vegetables in a colander, rinse and squeeze dry with a piece of muslin.
- Spread vegetables on a tray and leave to air in a sunny place for 1 hour.
- Repeat process with the mustard greens, using the remaining 2 tsp salt.
- Combine pickling mixture ingredients and boil in an enamel saucepan for 1 minute. Remove from heat to cool.
- Blend a few spoonfuls of the pickling mixture with the French mustard, then add in the rest of the pickling mixture.
- Put all the vegetables in a large porcelain jar or glass bottle, pour in the pickling mixture and stir to combine.
- Leave uncovered for 48 hours, then store in refrigerator for future use.

Note:
Keep at least one day before serving.

Sambal Udang Kering Goreng

FRIED DRIED PRAWNS

INGREDIENTS

Candlenut	6
Turmeric	20 g (1 Tbsp), peeled
Shrimp paste (*belacan*)	1 tsp
Sugar	6 Tbsp
Salt	$^1/_2$ Tbsp
Tamarind pulp (*asam*)	3 Tbsp, mixed with 140ml ($^2/_3$ cup) water, squeezed and strained
Dried prawns	340 g (12 oz), soaked and finely pounded
Cooking oil	285 ml (1$^1/_4$ cups)
Green chillies	115 g (4 oz), finely sliced
Red chillies	115 g (4 oz), finely sliced
Garlic	115 g (4 oz), peeled and finely sliced
Shallots	225 g (8 oz), peeled and finely sliced
Lemon grass	10 stalks, finely sliced slantwise

METHOD

- Combine candlenuts, turmeric and shrimp paste and pound to a paste.
- Add sugar, salt, tamarind water and dried prawns and mix thoroughly.
- Heat cooking oil in wok. Fry chillies, garlic, shallots and lemon grass separately until light brown. Remove and set aside.
- Leaving oil in the wok, fry the dried prawn mixture over low heat until almost dry.
- Return the fried ingredients to the wok. Stir-fry for 5 minutes and transfer to a tray to cool.

Note:
When using an electric blender, do not soak or wash the dried prawns. Blend a little at a time.

Stir the dried prawn mixture constantly when cooking to prevent burning.

The dish can be kept for months if stored in a refrigerator.

soup

NYONYA SPECIALTIES – THE BEST OF SINGAPORE'S RECIPES

Buah Paya Masak Titik

PAPAYA SOUP

INGREDIENTS

Prawns	340 g (12 oz), shelled (keep shells for stock)
Salt	A pinch
Sugar	A pinch
Water	900 ml (4 cups)
Dried prawns	55 g (2 oz), soaked and finely pounded
Salted fish bones	225 g (8 oz), cut into small pieces
Green papaya	1, about 900g (2 lb), skinned and diced
Sweet basil leaves (*daun kemangi*)	1 handful

Rempah

Candlenuts	3, crushed
Shrimp paste (*belacan*)	1 Tbsp
Shallots	85 g (3 oz), peeled
Red chilli	1
Peppercorn or ground pepper	1 Tbsp

Seasoning

Salt	1 tsp
Sugar	2 tsp
Chicken stock cube	1

METHOD

- Grind *rempah* ingredients into a fine paste.
- Marinade the prawns with salt and sugar.
- Prepare prawn stock: In a wok, fry prawn shells in 1 Tbsp cooking oil. When cooked, pound the fried shells, then boil in 900 ml (4 cups) water for 5 minutes. Strain and set stock aside.
- In an enamel saucepan, combine dried prawns, *rempah* paste, salted fish bones, seasoning and prawn stock. Bring to a boil, then add papaya. Boil over moderate heat until tender. Add prawns and cook for 2–3 minutes. Set aside.
- To serve, dish papaya soup into a large bowl. Garnish with sweet basil leaves and sprinkle 1 Tbsp lard. Serve hot.

Bak Wan Kepiting

MINCED PORK WITH CRAB AND BAMBOO SHOOT SOUP

INGREDIENTS

Meatballs

Minced pork	455 g (1 lb)
Fish paste (ready-to-use)	115 g (4 oz)
Crab meat	115 g (4 oz), steamed
Bamboo shoots	55 g (2 oz), boiled and finely shredded

Seasoning

Lard or cooking oil	1 Tbsp
Garlic	1 Tbsp, peeled, chopped and browned
Salt	1 tsp
Pepper	A pinch
MSG	1 tsp, optional
Egg	1
Sugar	1/2 tsp
Soy sauce	1 Tbsp

For the Soup

Lard or cooking oil	2 Tbsp
Garlic	1 tsp, peeled and finely chopped
Bamboo shoots	250 g (9 oz), boiled and thinly shredded
Water	2.5 litres (11 cups)
Chicken stock cube	1
Salt	1 level tsp
MSG	1 tsp, optional

METHOD

- Make the meatballs: Combine minced pork, fish paste, seasoning ingredients, crab meat and the 55 g (2 oz) bamboo shoots in a large bowl. Mix and set aside.
- For the soup: Heat the 2 Tbsp of lard or cooking oil in a saucepan. Add in the garlic and fry until light brown. Add the finely shredded bamboo shoots and fry for short while. Pour in 2.5 litres (11 cups) water and chicken stock cube and bring to a boil.
- Take spoonfuls of the meat mixture and form into balls the size of walnuts. Bring soup to a rapid boil and put in the meatballs. When meatballs float to surface, test one to see if cooked.
- Adjust seasoning and dish into serving bowls. Serve hot.

Itik Tim

SALTED CHINESE MUSTARD DUCK SOUP

INGREDIENTS

Salted Chinese mustard (*kiam chye*)	560 g (1 1/4 lb)
Duck	1, quartered
Brandy	1 Tbsp
Water	3.6 litres (16 cups)
Pork foreleg	625 g (1 lb 6 oz), cut into pieces
Tomatoes	4, quartered, optional

Aromatics

Dried sour fruit (*asam gelugur*)	4 slices
Ginger	2 thick slices, peeled
Salted plums	4

Seasoning

Brandy	1/2 Tbsp
Salt	2 tsp
MSG	1 tsp, optional

METHOD

- Cut salted mustard into large pieces and soak in water for 1/2 hour. Drain and set aside.
- Season the duck with brandy.
- In a large pot, boil 3.6 litres (16 cups) water. Add the duck, salted mustard and aromatics. When the water boils again, add seasoning ingredients and pork.
- Let the soup boil rapidly for 10 minutes. Lower the heat and leave to simmer until the meat is tender (about 1–1 1/2 hours).
- If using tomatoes, add them to the soup during the last 10 minutes of cooking. Serve hot.

Pong Tauhu

BEAN CURD WITH MEATBALL SOUP

INGREDIENTS

Prawns	625 g (1 lb 6 oz), shelled and deveined (keep shells)
Water	1.4 litres (6^1/$_2$ cups)
Firm bean curd (*taukwa*)	4 pieces, small
Bamboo shoots	625 g (1^1/$_2$ lb), boiled and sliced into fine strips
Streaky pork	300 g (11 oz)
Water	900 ml (4 cups)
Minced pork	625 g (1 lb 6 oz)
Spring onions	2 Tbsp, finely chopped
Lard or cooking oil	2 Tbsp
Garlic	1 tsp, peeled and pounded
Yellow bean paste (*taucheo*)	1 Tbsp, pounded
Sugar	1 tsp
Salt	1–1^1/$_2$ tsp
MSG	1 tsp, optional

Seasoning

Salt	1 Tbsp
MSG	1 tsp, optional
Egg	1
Dark soy sauce	1 tsp
Cooking oil	4 Tbsp
Garlic	1 Tbsp, peeled, minced and fried crisp
Pepper	1 tsp

METHOD

- Wash, drain and fry prawn shells. Pound the fried shells and mix with 1.4 litres (6^1/$_2$ cups) water. Strain and set aside prawn stock.
- Combine prawns and bean curd and mince finely. Set aside.
- Boil streaky pork in 900 ml (4 cups) water. Cut pork into fine strips. Set aside pork stock.
- Mix seasoning ingredients in a bowl. Add prawn-bean curd mixture, minced pork and spring onions. Grease hands and roll mixture into walnut-sized balls. Place the meatballs on a tray.
- Heat 2 Tbsp lard or cooking oil and fry pounded garlic until light brown.
- Add yellow bean paste and sugar and stir-fry for 1 minute. Add bamboo shoots and stir. Add prawn stock and pork stock, salt and MSG, if using. Boil for 15 minutes.
- Add meatballs and pork strips to boiling soup. Cook gently until meatballs float to the surface. Keep boiling for 5–7 minutes.
- Serve hot.

Tauhu Masak Titik

SPICY BEAN CURD AND SALTED FISH SOUP

INGREDIENTS

Penang salted fish bones	115 g (4 oz), cut into pieces
Water	900 ml (4 cups)
Cooking oil	4 Tbsp
Firm bean curd (taukwa)	1 piece, cut into 24 pieces
Chinese celery	4 sprigs, chopped

Meatballs

Pork	455 g (1 lb), minced
Prawns	455 g (1 lb), minced, keep shells
Salt	1/2 tsp
Sugar	1/2 tsp
MSG	1/2 tsp, optional
Soy sauce	1 tsp
Pepper	To taste

Rempah

Shallots	55 g (2 oz), peeled
Candlenuts	4, crushed
Red chilli	1, seeded
Shrimp paste (belacan)	1 Tbsp
Pepper	1/4 tsp

Seasoning for Stock

Salt	1 tsp
Chicken stock cube	1

METHOD

- Wash salted fish bones and drain.
- Combine *rempah* ingredients and pound to a fine paste.
- Wash and drain prawn shells, then fry in 1 Tbsp cooking oil until cooked.
- Place the fried shells in a saucepan with 900 ml (4 cups) water and boil for 10 minutes. Add seasoning, strain and set aside.
- In a large bowl, combine meatball ingredients and blend well by hand. Shape the mixture into candlenut-sized balls and set aside.
- Heat the remaining 3 Tbsp of cooking oil in a saucepan and fry *rempah* until fragrant. Pour in prawn stock and salted fish bones and bring to a boil.
- Add in meatballs and cook until well done. Add bean curd, bring to boil again for another 10 minutes, then remove saucepan from heat.
- Pour into a serving bowl and garnish with Chinese celery.

Stuffed Cuttlefish Soup

INGREDIENTS

Cuttlefish	300 g (11 oz), small
Water	680 ml (3 cups)
Cellophane noodles (*tang hoon*)	15 g (¹/₂ oz), soaked in hot water

Stuffing
Minced pork	310 g (11 oz)
Prawns	225 g (8 oz), shelled, deveined and finely diced
Salt	¹/₄ tsp
MSG	¹/₂ tsp, optional
Cornflour	¹/₄ tsp

Seasoning
Salt	1 tsp
MSG	1 tsp, optional
Chicken stock cube	1

Garnish
Chinese celery	2 sprigs
Garlic	2 cloves, peeled, chopped and fried
Pepper	To taste

METHOD

- Remove head, ink bag and cartilage from cuttlefish. Set aside the heads. Wash and clean the inside of the cuttlefish and drain.
- In a bowl, combine stuffing ingredients and mix thoroughly. Stuff each of the cuttlefish until three-quarter full. Re-attach head.
- Use the remaining stuffing mixture to shape into little meatballs.
- Boil 680 ml (3 cups) water in a saucepan. Add the stuffed cuttlefish and meatballs and boil for 3 minutes. Add seasoning ingredients. Cut up the cellophane noodles and add to the soup.
- Add garnish ingredients and serve in a large bowl.

Note:
When cleaning the cuttlefish, remove the brown outer skin so that the soup will remain clear. Before stuffing the cuttlefish, make a slit at the tail end to prevent the stuffing from spilling out during cooking.

Hee Peow Soup

FISH MAW SOUP

INGREDIENTS

Fried fish maw (*hee peow*)	115 g (4 oz)
Water	4.5 litres (20 cups)
Salt	1 tsp
MSG	1 tsp, optional
Fish balls (ready-to-use)	50
Cabbage	900 g (2 lb), cut into pieces
Chinese parsley (coriander leaves	55 g (2 oz), chopped
Crisp-fried shallots	(*Recipe on page 12*)
Pepper	To taste

Stock

Chicken	1 kg (2¼ lb), whole, washed and chopped
Water	3.5 litres (15½ cups)
Pork bones	455 g (1 lb), chopped into small pieces
Salt	1 tsp
Peppercorns	1 tsp

Prawn Balls

Fish paste (ready-to-use)	340 g (12 oz)
Prawns	150 g (5 oz), shelled and minced
Sugar	1 tsp
Salt	A pinch
Red food colouring	A few drops

Pork Balls

Minced pork	680 g (1½ lb)
Fish paste	340 g (12 oz), ready-to-use
Prawns	300 g (10 oz), shelled and minced
Salt	1 tsp
Sugar	1 tsp
MSG	1 tsp, optional
Pepper	¼ tsp
Dark soy sauce	1 tsp
Sesame oil	½ tsp
Cooking oil	2 Tbsp
Carrots	170 g (5 oz), skinned and finely shredded

METHOD

- Prepare fish maw: Scald fish maw with boiling water. When it is cool enough to handle, squeeze out the water from the fish maw, cut into small pieces and set aside.
- Prepare the stock: Wash and cut chicken into small pieces.
- In a saucepan, put 2.3 litres (10 cups) water and the rest of the stock ingredients and bring to the boil over high heat. Boil for 20 minutes, removing scum from time to time. Add the remaining 1.2 litres (5½ cups) of water and keep boiling and skimming surface until soup is free of scum. Reduce heat and boil for ½ hour. Strain; remove peppercorns and set stock aside.
- Prepare prawn balls: In a large bowl, combine the fish paste, minced prawns, sugar, salt and a few drops of the red food colouring.
- Take handfuls of the prawn paste and throw against the side of bowl 8–10 times. Form into candlenut-sized balls by squeezing dollops of the paste out between your index finger and thumb. Scoop out with a porcelain spoon dipped into cold water and drop into a basin of cold water. Set aside for ½ hour.
- Meanwhile, combine the minced pork with fish paste and minced prawns. Add the rest of the pork ball ingredients and mix by hand until well combined. Set aside.
- In a large saucepan, combine 4.5 litres (20 cups) of water, 1 tsp salt and 1 tsp MSG, if using, and bring to a rapid boil. Boil the balls in the following order: fish balls, prawn balls, meatballs. When cooked, transfer the balls to a large plate and set aside. Boil cabbage until tender.
- Leave cabbage in the saucepan and add chicken stock. Bring to the boil. Put in fish maw and boil for 1–2 minutes. Remove from heat.
- To serve: Put all ingredients into soup and bring to boil. Transfer into large serving bowl and garnish with Chinese parsley, crisp-fried shallots and a dash of pepper. Serve hot.

seafood

NYONYA SPECIALTIES – THE BEST OF SINGAPORE'S RECIPES

Asam Gulai

FISH IN SPICY TAMARIND GRAVY

INGREDIENTS

Dried sour fruit (*asam gelugur*)	2 slices
Sugar	1 Tbsp
Salt	A pinch
Lady's fingers	300 g (11 oz), trimmed and halved
Cooking oil	115 ml (½ cup)
Tamarind pulp (*asam*)	1–1½ Tbsp, mixed with 900 ml (4 cups) water, squeezed and strained
Prawns or fish head	625 g (1 lb 6 oz), trimmed and washed

Rempah

Lemon grass	3 stalks, thinly sliced
Turmeric	10 g (1 tsp), peeled
Dried chillies	20, or 2–3 Tbsp dried chilli paste (*recipe on page 13*)
Shallots	20, peeled
Garlic	2 cloves, peeled
Shrimp paste (*belacan*)	1 Tbsp

Seasoning

Sugar	2 Tbsp
Salt	2 tsp
MSG	½ tsp, optional
Torch ginger flower (*bunga kantan*)	2 stalks, halved lengthwise

METHOD

- In a saucepan, combine the dried sour fruit, sugar and pinch of salt with enough water to completely immerse the lady's fingers. Bring to a boil. Add the lady's fingers and boil for about 10–15 minutes or until tender. Drain and set aside.
- Pound or process the *rempah* ingredients to a fine paste.
- Heat 115 ml (½ cup) cooking oil in wok and fry the *rempah* until oil bubbles through, stirring constantly.
- Add the seasoning ingredients and some of the tamarind water. Cook for 1 minute, then add the rest of the tamarind water. Stir and bring to a boil. Cook for another 2 minutes, uncovered.
- Put in the prawns or fish head and cook until done. Finally, add the lady's fingers, heat through and serve.

Note:
To choose young and tender lady's fingers, bend the ends to see if they snap easily. Those that do not break easily are tough and stringy.

Goreng Ikan Terubuk

FISH IN SCREWPINE LEAVES

INGREDIENTS

Herring (*ikan terubuk*)	900 g (2 lb), whole or halved
Salt	1 tsp
Screwpine (*pandan*) leaves	6, washed
Cooking oil	225 ml (1 cup)

METHOD

- Wash the fish, rub it with the salt and leave to marinate for $1/2$ hour.
- Wrap the screwpine leaves round the fish.
- Heat cooking oil in a wok and fry fish over moderately high heat until crisp and brown on both sides.
- Remove the screwpine leaves and place the fish on a plate. Pour the hot oil over and serve hot.

Note:
Do not scale the fish. The fish should be fried over moderately high heat so that it is thoroughly cooked and the scales are crisp. Sprinkle some water while frying before covering the pan. The steam from the water will hasten the cooking.

Udang Kuah Pedas Nanas

PRAWNS IN PINEAPPLE GRAVY

INGREDIENTS

Water	900 ml (4 cups)
Salt	1 Tbsp
Sugar	1 Tbsp
Pineapple	1, skinned and cut into thin pieces
Dried sour fruit (*asam gelugur*)	2 slices
King prawns	625 g (1 lb 6 oz), washed and trimmed
Sweet basil leaves (*daun kemangi*)	A handful

Rempah

Galangal	14 slices, peeled
Turmeric	10 g (1 tsp), peeled
Shallots	115 g (4 oz), peeled
Red chillies	3
Shrimp paste (*belacan*)	1 Tbsp

METHOD

- Pound *rempah* ingredients, add the ingredients in the given order, to form a fine paste.
- Transfer the paste to an enamel saucepan. Add the water, salt, sugar, pineapple and dried sour fruit and mix. Boil over moderate heat for 10 minutes.
- Add the prawns and continue to boil uncovered for 2 minutes until cooked.
- Remove the pan from the heat. Garnish with basil leaves and serve hot.

Note:
The gravy can be boiled in advance. Add the prawns to cook just before serving so that the prawns will be sweet and tasty.

Sambal Udang

PRAWN SAMBAL

INGREDIENTS

Cooking oil	6 Tbsp
Coconut	170 g (6 oz), grated, squeezed with 115 ml (1/2 cup) water to extract No.2 coconut milk
Prawns	900 g (2 lbs), shelled, deveined and slit lengthwise

Rempah

Shallots	15, about 115 g (4 oz), peeled
Dried chillies	15
Fresh red chillies	10, seeded
Garlic	1 clove, peeled
Candlenuts	4, crushed
Lemon grass	1 stalk, thinly sliced

Seasoning

Sugar	1 tsp
Salt	1/2 tsp
MSG	A pinch, optional
Tamarind pulp (*asam*)	1 Tbsp, mixed with 55 ml (1/4 cup) water, squeezed and strained

METHOD

- Grind *rempah* ingredients into a fine paste.
- Add cooking oil to a heated wok. When oil is hot, fry the *rempah* paste over moderate heat until oil bubbles through. Add some coconut milk as you fry.
- Add prawns and seasoning ingredients and stir-fry for 2 minutes. Add remaining coconut milk and cook until sauce thickens.
- Serve.

Prawn Salad

INGREDIENTS

Coconut	455 g (1 lb), skinned and grated
Cucumber	1
Lettuce	115 g (4 oz)
Shallots	4, peeled and thinly sliced
Red chilli	1, seeded, thinly sliced lengthwise
Crisp-fried shallots	(*Recipe on page 12*)

For Prawns

Water	800 ml (3^1/$_2$ cups)
Salt	1 Tbsp
Sugar	1 Tbsp
Cooking oil	1 Tbsp
Prawns	600 g (1 lb 5 oz), washed and drained

Dressing

Kaffir lime leaves (*daun limau purut*)	2, central vein removed
Red chillies	2, seeded
Shrimp paste (*belacan*)	1 Tbsp, roasted
Sugar	1 tsp
Salt	^{1}/$_2$ tsp
Lemon juice	2 tsp

METHOD

- Prepare the prawns: In a pan, combine 800 ml (3^1/$_2$ cups) water, the salt, sugar and cooking oil and bring to a boil. Add the prawns and cook over moderately high heat for 5–7 minutes or until prawns are cooked.
- Remove prawns and soak in cold water for 10 minutes. Shell prawns, devein and set aside.
- Make the dressing. Pound the kaffir lime leaves, chillies and shrimp paste together. Transfer to a bowl and blend in sugar, salt and lemon juice. Set aside.
- Use a muslin cloth and squeeze grated coconut to extract No.1 milk.
- Place milk in a pan together with a pinch of salt and boil gently until thick and creamy. Set aside to cool.
- Skin cucumber and cut into 4, lengthwise. Remove the seeds and slice thickly. Chill.
- Shred lettuce and chill in iced water until ready for use. Drain and roll lettuce in a tea towel to dry.
- Assemble the salad: Place cucumber, sliced raw shallots and lettuce in a large bowl with the shrimp paste mixture and one-third of the coconut cream. Mix. Place the salad on a serving plate, pour over with remaining coconut cream and top with prawns, sliced chilli and crisp-fried shallots. Serve.

Ikan Masak Asam Pekat

FISH IN TAMARIND JUICE

INGREDIENTS

Spotted Spanish mackerel (*ikan tenggiri papan*)	625 g (1 lb 6 oz), scaled, washed and deboned
Tamarind pulp *(asam)*	170 g (6 oz), mixed with 340ml (1 1/2 cups) water, squeezed and strained
Red chillies	6, slit lengthwise
Green chillies	6, slit lengthwise
Lard or cooking oil	1 tsp

Rempah

Turmeric	20 g, peeled, or 1 tsp ground turmeric
Shrimp paste (*belacan*)	2 Tbsp
Shallots	8, about 55 g (2 oz), peeled

Marinade

Sugar	1 tsp
Salt	1/2 tsp
Tamarind pulp *(asam)*	1 Tbsp, seeded
Water	115 ml (1/2 cup)

Seasoning

Sugar	6 Tbsp
Salt	1 1/2 tsp

METHOD

- Combine *rempah* ingredients and grind or blend into a fine paste.
- Cut fish into 2.5-cm (1-in) cubes.
- Combine marinade ingredients and marinate fish for 1/2 hour. Drain.
- Pour tamarind water into an enamel saucepan, add seasoning ingredients and *rempah* paste and boil gently for 15 minutes.
- Add in fish, red and green chillies and cook for another 5–7 minutes or until fish is done.
- Stir in the lard or cooking oil and remove from heat. Serve hot or at room temperature.

Sambal Sotong

HOT SPICY CUTTLEFISH

INGREDIENTS

Cooking oil	2 Tbsp
Onions	170 g (6 oz), peeled and sliced
Tomatoes	2, cut into wedges
Chilli garam paste	2–3 Tbsp (*recipe on page 158*)
Red chilli	1, seeded and thickly sliced
Green chillies	2, seeded and thickly sliced

For Cuttlefish

Cuttlefish (*sotong karang*)	300 g (11 oz)
Sugar	1 tsp
Salt	$1/4$ tsp

For Cucumber

Cucumber	1
Salt	$1/2$ tsp

Gravy

Tomato sauce	2 Tbsp
Sugar	1 tsp
MSG	$1/2$ tsp, optional
Pepper	$1/4$ tsp
Vinegar	2 tsp
Water	3 Tbsp
Tapioca flour or cornflour	1 tsp

METHOD

- Prepare the cuttlefish: Wash cuttlefish, remove head, black ink bag and centre cartilage. Cut into 1-cm ($1/2$ -in) rings, season with sugar and salt and set aside.
- Prepare the cucumber: Quarter cucumber lengthwise and remove seeds. Cut diagonally into small pieces and rub with salt. Set aside.
- Prepare the gravy mixture: In a bowl, combine all gravy ingredients and set aside.
- Heat cooking oil in a wok and stir-fry the onions and tomatoes. Increase heat and add cuttlefish, chilli garam paste and gravy mixture. Stir, cover wok and cook for 5 minutes.
- Remove lid, add the sliced chillies and cucumber and heat through.
- Serve.

poultry

NYONYA SPECIALTIES – THE BEST OF SINGAPORE'S RECIPES

Ayam Buah Keluak

CHICKEN IN BLACK NUT CURRY

INGREDIENTS

Garam asam paste	340 g (1¹/₄ lb), thawed *(recipe on page 158)*
Pork ribs	570 g (20 oz), cut into pieces

For the Black Nut

Indonesian black nuts (*buah keluak*)	30
Salt	A pinch
Sugar	¹/₂ tsp

For the Chicken

Chicken	1.4 kg (3 lb), cut into pieces
Salt	1 tsp
MSG	1 tsp, optional

Sauce

Tamarind pulp (*asam*)	85 g (3 oz), mixed with 170 ml (³/₄ cup) water, squeezed and strained
Salt	1–1¹/₂ tsp
MSG	1 tsp, optional
Water	900 ml (4 cups)

METHOD

- To prepare the black nut: Soak nuts in cold water for ¹/₂ hour. Scrub nuts to remove sandy particles, then crack open where the nut is smooth. Remove meat of the nut and combine with a pinch of salt and ¹/₂ tsp sugar. Pound or process together to form a firm, smooth paste. Stuff it back into the shells and set aside.
- Meanwhile, marinate chicken with 1 tsp salt and 1 tsp MSG, if using. Leave for at least ¹/₂ hour.
- Place the thawed garam asam paste in a pan with the sauce ingredients and bring to the boil over high heat. Add pork ribs and boil for 5 minutes. Reduce heat to moderate and cook for ¹/₂ hour.
- Add the prepared nuts and then the chicken and continue cooking for another ¹/₂ hour or until chicken is tender, stirring occasionally.
- Serve with white rice.

Ayam Goreng Asam

FRIED TAMARIND CHICKEN

INGREDIENTS

Chicken	1.2 kg (2 lb 11 oz), quartered
Cooking oil for deep-frying	

Marinade

Tamarind pulp (*asam*)	3 Tbsp
Salt	1 1/2 tsp
Sugar	3 tsp
MSG	1 tsp, optional
Pepper	1 tsp
Soy sauce	2 tsp
Water	8 Tbsp

METHOD

- Combine marinade ingredients in a bowl.
- Wash chicken and wipe with kitchen towel until very dry.
- Prick chicken all over with a fork and rub all over with marinade. Leave aside for 45 minutes.
- In a heated wok, add cooking oil and heat until very hot.
- Now add chicken and reduce heat to moderate. Fry until light brown, dry and crispy on both sides. Turn heat to low if chicken browns too quickly.
- When done, transfer to a serving plate.

Note:
To prevent chicken from getting too oily, keep cooking oil at boiling point while frying.

Ayam Kleo

CHICKEN IN RICH SPICY GRAVY

INGREDIENTS

Chicken	1.2 kg (2 lb 11 oz), quartered
Coconut	625 g (1 lb 6 oz), grated
Water	430 ml (1³/₄ cups)

Rempah
Dried chillies	4
Red chillies	2
Lemon grass	1 stalk, thinly sliced
Candlenuts	6, crushed
Ginger	1 Tbsp, peeled
Turmeric	¹/₂ tsp, peeled
Garlic	3 cloves, peeled
Shallots	15, peeled

Marinade for Chicken
Salt	1 tsp
MSG	1 tsp, optional
Water	2 Tbsp

Seasoning
Salt	1 tsp
MSG	¹/₂ tsp, optional
Dried sour fruit (asam gelugur)	1 slice
Kaffir lime leaves (daun limau purut)	5
Lemon grass	2 stalks, lightly crushed

METHOD

- Pound or process rempah ingredients together to make a fine paste.
- Marinate chicken with marinade ingredients and 2 Tbsp of rempah paste for at least ¹/₂ hour.
- Combine grated coconut and water. Using a piece of muslin, squeeze coconut to extract No.2 milk. Collect.
- Set grill to hot. Grill the marinated chicken until brown on both sides (10 minutes for each side).
- In a saucepan, combine the remaining rempah paste, coconut milk and seasoning ingredients. Add in the chicken and mix well.
- Cook over moderate heat for 15 minutes. Reduce heat and let chicken simmer until tender, and the gravy is thick.

Ayam Merah

CHICKEN IN RED SPICY SAUCE

INGREDIENTS

Chicken	1.2 kg (2¹/₂ lb), cut into large pieces
Coconut	455 g (1 lb), grated
Water	280 ml (1¹/₂ cups)
Cooking oil	4 Tbsp
Kaffir lime leaves (*daun limau purut*)	10
Lemon grass	2 stalks, crushed
Salt	1 Tbsp
MSG	¹/₂ tsp, optional
Tamarind pulp (*asam*)	30 g (1 oz), mixed with 115ml (¹/₂ cup) water, squeezed and strained

Rempah

Candlenuts	10
Ginger	¹/₂ tsp, peeled
Chilli powder	2 Tbsp
Red chillies	10, seeded
Red bird's eye chillies (*cili padi*)	10
Garlic	1 clove, peeled
Shrimp paste (*belacan*)	1 tsp
Shallots	55 g (2 oz), peeled

Marinade for Chicken

Sugar	1 Tbsp
Salt	1 tsp
MSG	1 tsp, optional

METHOD

- Pound or process *rempah* ingredients to a fine paste and set aside.
- Marinate chicken with marinade ingredients for ¹/₂ hour.
- Using a muslin cloth, squeeze coconut for No.1 milk and collect in a bowl. Set aside.
- Add 280 ml (1¹/₄ cups) water to coconut and squeeze again into a separate bowl for No.2 milk. Set aside.
- Grease a roasting pan with 2 Tbsp cooking oil. Rub chicken with the remaining 2 Tbsp oil and roast chicken in a hot oven until light brown, turning at least once. Remove from oven and set aside.
- Place No.2 milk, *rempah*, kaffir lime leaves and lemon grass into a heated pan and boil over medium heat for 10 minutes. Season with 1 Tbsp salt and ¹/₂ tsp MSG, if using.
- Add roasted chicken, pan juices and tamarind water and boil for another 10 minutes.
- Pour in No.1 milk, reduce heat and simmer uncovered for l0–12 minutes or until chicken is tender.
- Remove from heat and serve.

Ayam Sioh

CHICKEN IN THICK SPICY TAMARIND SAUCE

INGREDIENTS

Chicken	1.6 kg (3¹/₂ lb), quartered
Salt	2 Tbsp
Tamarind pulp (*asam*)	225 g (8 oz), mixed with 340ml (1¹/₂ cups) water, squeezed and strained
Cooking oil	

Seasoning

Ground coriander	3 Tbsp, roasted
Sugar	10 Tbsp
Salt	1 Tbsp
Dark soy sauce	2 Tbsp
Pepper	1 rounded tsp
Shallots	170 g (6 oz), peeled and finely pounded

METHOD

- Wash chicken in water mixed with salt. Drain.
- In a deep bowl, combine seasoning ingredients and tamarind water.
- Add chicken pieces. Cover and leave to marinate overnight or at least 10 hours.
- Transfer chicken and marinade to a saucepan and cook for 20 minutes over moderate heat.
- Reduce heat to low and cook for another 20–30 minutes or until chicken is very tender. Set aside to cool.
- Heat some cooking oil in a pan and fry chicken pieces. Serve.

Ayam Tempra

SPICY CHICKEN

INGREDIENTS

Chicken	900 g (2 lb), cut into pieces
Cooking oil	5 Tbsp
Onions	225 g (8 oz), peeled and cut into rings
Green chillies	8, thickly sliced
Red chillies	6, thickly sliced

Marinade for Chicken

Salt	1 tsp
MSG	1 tsp, optional

Seasoning

Dark soy sauce	1 Tbsp
Sugar	1 Tbsp
Salt	$1/2$ tsp
MSG	$1/2$ tsp, optional
Lime juice	2 tsp
Water	225 ml (1 cup)

METHOD

- Rub chicken with marinade ingredients and set aside for $1/2$ hour.
- Combine seasoning ingredients in another bowl.
- Heat a wok until very hot, then add 4 Tbsp cooking oil. When hot, add onions and chillies and fry for $1/2$ minute.
- Add the chicken and stir-fry over high heat until cooked, about 7 minutes.
- Add seasoning ingredients and cook for another 5 minutes.
- Lower the heat, cover wok and cook gently for 20 minutes or until chicken is tender.
- Remove lid, add the last tablespoon of oil, stir and serve.

Kari Ayam

CHICKEN CURRY

INGREDIENTS

Chicken	1, about 1.6 kg (3¹/₂ lb), cut into pieces
Coconut	455 g (1 lb), grated
Water	570 ml (2¹/₂ cups)
Corn oil	5 Tbsp
Curry powder	55 g (2 oz)
Curry leaves	1 sprig

Marinade for Chicken

Curry powder	30 g (1 oz)
Salt	1 tsp
Sugar	1 tsp
MSG	1 tsp, optional

Rempah

Shallots	85 g (3 oz), peeled
Garlic	3 cloves, peeled
Ginger	10 g, peeled and thinly sliced
Shrimp paste (*belacan)*	1 tsp

METHOD

- Season chicken with marinade ingredients for ¹/₂ hour.
- Using a piece of muslin, squeeze grated coconut for No.1 milk. Collect milk in a bowl and set aside. Add the water to the grated coconut and squeeze again to extract No.2 milk. Collect in a separate bowl and set aside.
- Grind *rempah* ingredients to a rough paste.
- Heat corn oil in a wok and fry *rempah* paste until oil separates and mixture turns light brown.
- Add in the 55 g (2 oz) curry powder, curry leaves and half of the No.1 milk. Stir until oil separates and takes on a red hue. Add in the rest of the No.1 milk and bring to a boil, stirring continuously to prevent burning.
- Add in chicken and cook over moderate heat, stirring occasionally.
- Reduce heat to low, cover the wok and simmer for 20–25 minutes or until chicken is tender.
- Add in some of the No.2 milk to get desired thickness for the gravy. (Make a thinner gravy if it is to be eaten with bread and a thicker gravy if it is to be eaten with rice.) Simmer for another 5–7 minutes, remove from heat and serve.

Enche Kebin

CRISPY CURRIED CHICKEN

INGREDIENTS

Chicken	1, cut into pieces, or 900 g (2 lb) chicken wings
Cooking oil for deep-frying	
Cucumber	1, sliced
Tomatoes	2, sliced

Marinade

Sugar	2 Tbsp
Evaporated milk	1 Tbsp
Curry powder	1 Tbsp
Ginger juice	2 Tbsp, or 1 tsp ground ginger
Soy sauce	4 tsp
Pepper	1 tsp
MSG	1 tsp, optional

METHOD

- Wash the chicken and wipe dry.
- Mix marinade ingredients in a bowl and rub all over chicken. Set aside for 1 hour.
- Place chicken in the sun to dry thoroughly.
- Heat cooking oil in a pan until smoking hot. Put in the chicken and deep-fry for 2 minutes. Lower the heat and cook until golden brown. Transfer to a plate.
- Garnish with cucumber and tomatoes and serve hot.

meat

Babi Asam

PORK BRAISED IN TAMARIND SAUCE

INGREDIENTS

Cooking oil	4 Tbsp
Yellow bean paste (*taucheo*)	2 Tbsp, pounded
Belly pork	570 g (1¼ lb), cut into thick strips
Tamarind pulp (*asam*)	30 g (1 oz), mixed with 285 ml (1¼ cups) water, squeezed and strained
Green chillies	8, slit halfway lengthwise
Red chillies	6, slit halfway lengthwise

Rempah
Candlenuts	4, crushed
Shallots	90 g (3 oz), peeled
Shrimp paste (*belacan*)	1 Tbsp

Seasoning
Salt	½ tsp
Chicken stock cube	1
Sugar	2 Tbsp

METHOD

- Finely pound together *rempah* ingredients. Heat cooking oil in a wok and fry *rempah* paste until fragrant and light brown.
- Add yellow bean paste, seasoning ingredients and stir over low heat.
- Add in pork and half of the tamarind water. When pork begins to change colour, add red and green chillies and the remaining tamarind water.
- Bring to a boil, reduce heat and simmer until pork is tender – about 45 minutes to 1 hour.
- While cooking, add a little water if gravy is too thick. Serve hot.

Babi Chin

PORK BRAISED IN DARK SOY SAUCE

INGREDIENTS

Sugarcane *BAMBOO SHOOT*	2 x 30-cm ($^3/_4$ x 12-in) sticks, skinned
Cooking oil for frying	
Shallots	115 g (4 oz), peeled and coarsely pounded
Garlic	30 g (1 oz), peeled and coarsely pounded
Cinnamon quill	5-cm (2-in) piece
Yellow bean paste (*taucheo*)	3 Tbsp, finely pounded
Ground coriander	1 Tbsp
Water	850 ml (3$^3/_4$ cups)
Shoulder pork (with skin on)	1.4 kg (3 lb), cleaned and cut into 4-cm (1$^1/_2$-in) cubes
Chinese mushrooms	85 g (3 oz)
Bamboo shoots	455 g (1 lb), boiled and cut into thick wedges

Seasoning

Sugar	2 Tbsp
Salt	1 tsp
Dark soy sauce	2 tsp

METHOD

- Halve ~~sugarcane~~ B SHOOT lengthwise and cut again into 8-cm (3$^1/_4$-in) lengths.
- Heat some cooking oil in non-stick wok. Fry shallots, garlic and cinnamon quill until brown, add yellow bean paste, coriander and seasoning. Stir-fry for 2 minutes, add 425 ml (1$^3/_4$ cups) water and ~~sugarcane~~ B.S. and bring to a boil.
- Turn the heat up to high and add the pork. Cook until sauce is almost dry, stirring occasionally. Add in the remaining 425 ml (1$^3/_4$ cups) water and stir until gravy starts to boil. Keep boiling for 5 minutes.
- Add the mushrooms and bamboo shoots. Reduce heat, cover pan and simmer until pork is tender. Stir occasionally to prevent burning.
- Add a little water if gravy becomes too thick while cooking. Serve hot.

Babi Pong Tay

STEWED PORK

INGREDIENTS

Cooking oil	6 Tbsp
Shallots	115 g (4 oz), peeled and coarsely pounded
Garlic	4 cloves, peeled and coarsely pounded
Cinnamon quill	8-cm (3-in) piece
Shoulder of pork	625 g (1 lb 6 oz), cut into pieces
Pig's trotters	625 g (1 lb 6 oz), cut into pieces
Water	450 ml (2 cups)

Seasoning

Yellow bean paste (*taucheo*)	2 Tbsp, pounded
Sugar	1 Tbsp
Salt	1 tsp
Dark soy sauce	1 tsp

METHOD

- Heat cooking oil in wok and fry shallots, garlic and cinnamon quill until brown. Add seasoning ingredients and stir-fry for $1/2$ minute.
- Add in meat and 150 ml ($2/3$ cup) water and cook over high heat, stirring occasionally until almost dry – about $1/2$ hour.
- Now, add the remaining 300 ml ($1^1/3$ cups) water and bring to a rapid boil for 5 minutes.
- Transfer to a heavy bottomed saucepan, cover and let simmer for $1-1^1/2$ hours or until meat is tender. Serve hot or at room temperature.

Note:
This is an ideal picnic dish eaten with French loaf. Add more hot water when meat is tender, for more gravy.

Satay Babi

GRILLED SPICY PORK SKEWERS AND PEANUT SAUCE

Satay Babi

INGREDIENTS

Coconut	225 g (8 oz), grated
Pork	680 g (1¹/₂ lb), cut into 1.5-cm (¹/₂-in) thick slices
Cooking oil	85 ml (¹/₃ cup)

Rempah

Lemon grass	4 stalks, thinly sliced
Red chillies	4, seeded
Dried chillies	10, seeded
Candlenuts	4, crushed
Shrimp paste (*belacan*)	1 tsp
Shallots	15, peeled

Seasoning

Salt	1 tsp
MSG	¹/₂ tsp, optional
Pepper	¹/₂ tsp
Sugar	2 tsp
Cooking oil	3 Tbsp

METHOD

- Place coconut in a piece of 1 muslin and squeeze to extract No.1 milk. Collect in a container and set aside.
- Combine *rempah* ingredients and pound to a fine paste.
- Add seasoning ingredients and No.1 milk to *rempah* paste and mix. Rub this paste all over the pork and leave to marinate for 1 hour.
- Thread the meat through wooden or metal skewers. Brush with cooking oil and cook under a preheated hot grill until done.
- Serve with garnish ingredients and peanut sauce (*recipe on the right*) and/or pineapple sauce (*recipe on page 93*).

Note:
The marinated meat can also be fried over high heat in a wok until almost dry and the oil separates. Chicken can also be used instead of pork.

Peanut Sauce

INGREDIENTS

Peanuts	455g (1 lb), roasted and ground
Water	900 ml (4 cups)
Cooking oil	225 ml (1 cup)

Rempah

Shallots	15, peeled
Garlic	8 cloves, peeled
Lemon grass	2 stalks, thinly sliced
Dried chillies	20–30, seeded, or 4–5 Tbsp dried chilli paste (*recipe on page 13*)
Galangal	4 slices, peeled

Seasoning

Salt	2 Tbsp
Sugar	8–10 Tbsp
Lime juice	4 Tbsp, or 4 Tbsp thick tamarind water

Garnish

Cucumbers	2, wedged
Onions	2, peeled and wedged

METHOD

- Combine *rempah* ingredients and pound into a fine paste.
- In a saucepan, combine peanuts and water and bring to a boil over low heat. Stir constantly for about ¹/₂ hour until thick. Set aside.
- Heat cooking oil in a wok and fry *rempah* paste until fragrant and oil separates.
- Add *rempah* paste to the peanuts, followed by the seasoning ingredients. Bring to a boil over low heat for about 5–7 minutes. Stir constantly until sugar has dissolved.
- Remove from heat, cool and serve on the side with satay.
- Garnish with cucumber and onion wedges.

Pineapple Sauce

This variation can be served on the side on its own or mixed with the peanut sauce.

INGREDIENTS

Pineapple	1, small ripe

METHOD

- Skin pineapple and remove 'eyes'.
- Scrape pineapple meat into a bowl, leaving out the hard core.
- Drain off excess juice and serve.

Dry Beef Rendang

INGREDIENTS

Topside beef	670 g (1 1/2 lb), cubed
Coconut	570 g (1 1/4 lb), grated
Water	285 ml (1 1/4 cups)
Cooking oil	4 Tbsp
Kaffir lime leaves (*daun limau purut*)	4

Marinade for Beef

Salt	1 tsp
Sugar	1 tsp
Dark soy sauce	1 tsp

Rempah

Shallots	115 g (4 oz), peeled
Lemon grass	2 stalks, thinly sliced
Galangal	1 Tbsp, thinly sliced
Red chillies	4, seeded
Ginger	4 slices, peeled
Garlic	2 cloves, peeled
Candlenuts	4, crushed
Dried chillies	20, soaked, seeded
Shrimp paste (*belacan*)	1 tsp

Seasoning for Gravy

Salt	1 1/2 tsp
Sugar	2 tsp
MSG	1/2 tsp, optional
Dark soy sauce	1 tsp

METHOD

- Marinate beef with marinade ingredients for 1/2 hour.
- Combine *rempah* ingredients and pound to a fine paste. Set aside.
- Take 3 Tbsp grated coconut from the 570 g (20 oz) and toast in a pan until brown. While it is still hot, pound it finely and set aside.
- In a bowl, combine 115 ml (1/2 cup) water to the rest of the grated coconut. Using a piece of muslin, squeeze the coconut to extract No.1 coconut milk. Set aside.
- Add the remaining 170 ml (3/4 cup) water to coconut and squeeze to extract No.2 milk. Collect in a separate bowl and set aside.
- Heat a wok until hot. Add the cooking oil and when hot, put in the kaffir lime leaves and *rempah* paste. Stir over medium heat until oil bubbles through.
- Add in half of the No.1 milk, and stir until it boils. Then add beef and gravy seasoning. Cook uncovered for 45 minutes until almost dry, stirring occasionally.
- Add the remaining No.1 milk and stir well, cover pan and simmer until meat is tender – about 40 minutes.
- Now put in the toasted coconut and continue cooking until almost dry.
- Add some No.2 coconut milk for more gravy if preferred.
- Transfer to a plate and serve.

Char Bak

FRIED PORK, KIDNEY AND LIVER IN YELLOW BEAN PASTE

INGREDIENTS

Pig kidneys	1 pair, large, inner veins removed
Cooking oil or lard	2 Tbsp
Ginger	1 Tbsp, peeled and thinly shredded
Garlic	30 g (1 oz), peeled and finely pounded
Yellow bean paste (*taucheo*)	2 Tbsp, pounded
Sugar	1 tsp
MSG	1/2 tsp, optional
Pork tenderloin	285 g (10 oz), thinly sliced
Water	85 ml (1/3 cup)
Pig liver	225 g (8 oz), thinly sliced
Spring onions	3, cut into 1-cm (1/2-in) lengths
Brandy	1 Tbsp

METHOD

- To prepare kidneys: Score kidney surface in criss-cross pattern, then slice slantwise into bite-size pieces.
- Soak in cold water for 4–5 hours until kidneys double in size and is firm to the touch. Drain and scald with boiling water just before cooking.
- Heat cooking oil or lard in a wok. Add ginger and garlic and fry until light brown. Add yellow bean paste and sugar, and stir-fry over low heat for a moment. Add MSG, if using.
- Now add sliced pork and stir-fry until pork changes colour. Add water and bring to boil. Put in liver and cook for 1/2 minute, then add the prepared kidneys and spring onions. Stir-fry for 5 minutes, then add brandy.
- Transfer to a plate and serve hot.

Hati Babi Bungkus

MEAT AND LIVER BALLS

INGREDIENTS

Cooking oil	4 Tbsp
Shallots	15, peeled and finely pounded
Pork	300 g (11 oz), minced
Pork liver	300 g (11 oz), boiled and finely diced
Pepper	2 tsp
Ground coriander	2 Tbsp, roasted
Pork membrane	455 g (1 lb), cleaned and cut into 15-cm (6-in) squares

Seasoning

Sugar	3 Tbsp
Salt	1 tsp
Dark soy sauce	2 Tbsp
Vinegar	2 Tbsp

METHOD

To make meatballs

- Heat cooking oil in pan and fry pounded shallots until light brown. Reduce heat to low.
- Add seasoning ingredients and fry for $1/2$ minute.
- Transfer shallot mixture to a large bowl. Add the minced pork, liver, pepper and ground coriander. Knead well with hands to mix thoroughly.
- Form meat mixture into balls the size of a walnut. Place on a tray.
- Wrap each meatball tightly with a piece of pork membrane, overlapping several times to prevent the meat from coming out of the wrapper during frying.
- Heat a flat-bottomed frying pan half-filled with cooking oil.
- Place the meatballs, sealed end downwards, and fry over a moderate heat until brown. Turn over once.
- Serve.

Note:
Always boil the liver until half cooked, so that it will bind well with the minced meat. Always insist on fresh pig's membrane and wash carefully to remove dirt and bristle. Squeeze membrane lightly to drain excess water.

Tow Yew Bak

STREAKY BELLY PORK IN SOY SAUCE

INGREDIENTS

Streaky belly pork (with skin)	455 g (1 lb)
Salt	1/2 tsp
Dark soy sauce	1 Tbsp
Lard or cooking oil	2 Tbsp
Sugar	2 Tbsp
Star anise	2 petals
Garlic	2 cloves, peeled and lightly crushed
Soy sauce	2 Tbsp
MSG	1/2 tsp, optional
Water	230 ml (1 cup), hot

METHOD

- Scrape pork skin of bristles, wash and drain. Rub salt and dark soy sauce into pork and leave for 1/2 hour.
- Heat lard or cooking oil in a heavy-bottomed saucepan, add sugar and caramelize. Add star anise and garlic and fry for 1 minute. Add in the prepared pork, soy sauce and MSG, if using, and continue cooking for 2 minutes.
- Turn pork over, pour in half the hot water and boil over moderately high heat for 1/2 hour. Add remaining water, cover saucepan and cook over low heat for 45 minutes or until pork is tender.
- Lift pork onto a chopping board and slice. Place pork on a deep plate. Pour gravy over and serve.

Beef Serondeng

BEEF WITH GRATED COCONUT

INGREDIENTS

Water	115 ml (1/2 cup)
Rump or Scotch steak	560 g (1 1/4 lb), cut into pieces
Cooking oil	6 Tbsp
Coconut	560 g (1 1/4 lb), skinned and coarsely grated

Rempah

Galangal	6 slices, peeled
Shallots	14, peeled
Coriander seeds	4 Tbsp
Cumin seeds	1 tsp
Ginger	4 slices, peeled
Garlic	3 cloves, peeled
Turmeric	2 slices, peeled
Pepper	1 tsp

Seasoning

Salt	1 Tbsp
Sugar	5 Tbsp
Palm sugar (*gula Melaka*)	3 Tbsp, grated
Tamarind pulp (*asam*)	55 g (2 oz), mixed with 8 Tbsp water, squeezed and strained

METHOD

• Pound *rempah* ingredients to a paste.
• Bring the 115 ml (1/2 cup) of water to a boil in a pan. Add beef, one-third of the *rempah* paste and simmer until beef is tender and almost dry. Set aside.
• Heat 4 Tbsp of cooking oil in a wok and stir-fry the remaining *rempah* paste until fragrant.
• Add seasoning ingredients, stir-fry for a minute more and transfer to a dish. Rub fried paste into the grated coconut.
• Heat the remaining 2 Tbsp oil in a pan. Add the coconut mixture and the beef. Stir-fry over a low heat until moist and fragrant. (Keep stirring to prevent the coconut from burning.)
• When done, transfer to a plate and serve.

vegetables

NYONYA SPECIALTIES – THE BEST OF SINGAPORE'S RECIPES

Chap Chye Masak Titik

STEWED VEGETABLES NYONYA STYLE

INGREDIENTS

Belly pork	250 g (9 oz)
Salt	1/4 tsp
Water	750 ml (3 1/2 cups)
Prawns	250 g (9 oz)
Cloud ear fungus (*bok nee*)	30 g (1 oz), soaked in warm water
Golden needles (*kim chiam*)	60 g (2 oz)
Cellophane noodles (*tang hoon*)	30 g (1 oz), soaked in boiling water
Bean curd skin strips (*foo chok*)	60 g (2 oz), soaked in cold water for 10 minutes
Cooking oil	6 Tbsp
Sweet bean curd strips (*thim chok*)	10
Yellow bean paste (*taucheo*)	2 Tbsp, pounded
Cabbage	600 g (1 lb 5 oz), sliced
Dried Chinese mushrooms	60 g (2 oz), soaked in hot water

Rempah

Shallots	120 g (4 oz), peeled
Candlenuts	4, crushed
Red chilli	1
Shrimp paste (*belacan*)	2 Tbsp

Seasoning

Salt	1 tsp
MSG	1 tsp, optional
Sugar	2 tsp

METHOD

- Place pork in a saucepan together with 1/4 tsp salt and 500 ml (2 1/4 cups) water and boil for 20 minutes. Slice thinly and set aside. Reserve stock.
- Shell and devein prawns. Pound shells finely, stir in the remaining 250 ml (1 1/4 cups) water and strain. Set stock aside.
- Wash cloud ear fungus thoroughly to remove grit. Cut away the rough patch at the base and set aside.
- Cut off hard tops of golden needles, wash and drain. Cut cellophane noodles into short lengths. Soak bean curd skin strips in cold water for 10 minutes. Drain.
- Combine *rempah* ingredients and pound to a fine paste. Set aside.
- Heat a wok. Add cooking oil and fry sweet bean curd strips over low heat until they blister and turn light brown. Remove immediately and set aside.
- In the same pan, fry the *rempah* paste over moderate heat until fragrant. Add yellow bean paste and seasoning and stir-fry for 2 minutes.
- Then add prawns and prawn stock and bring to a boil.
- Put in cabbage, cook over high heat for 5 minutes, then pour in pork stock and remaining ingredients. Continue cooking for another 15–20 minutes or until cabbage is tender. Serve hot.

Nyonya Salad

INGREDIENTS

Kaffir lime leaf (*daun limau purut*)	1
Salt	1 tsp
Red chillies	2–3
Shrimp paste (*belacan*)	2 Tbsp, toasted
Vinegar	2–3 Tbsp
Sugar	$1/2$–1 Tbsp
Lime juice	1 tsp
Cucumbers	2, skin on, diced into 1-cm ($1/2$-in) cubes
Pineapple	$1/2$, skinned and diced into 1-cm ($1/2$-in) cubes
Dried prawns	4 Tbsp, soaked to soften and pounded

METHOD

- Make the dressing: Pound together kaffir lime leaf and salt. Add red chillies and shrimp paste and pound to a fine paste. Transfer to a dish.
- Add in vinegar, sugar and lime juice and stir to blend. Set aside.
- Place the cucumber and pineapple cubes in a large bowl. Add dried prawns and mix thoroughly.
- Add dressing, stir thoroughly and serve.

Rebung Masak Lemak

BAMBOO SHOOTS IN SPICY COCONUT GRAVY

INGREDIENTS

Coconut	455 g (1 lb), grated
Water	900 ml (4 cups)
Cooking oil	115 ml ($^{1}/_{2}$ cup)
Lemon grass	2 stalks, bruised
Bamboo shoots	455 g (1 lb) boiled and thinly sliced
Chicken	900 g (2 lb), cut into pieces
Pork ribs	340 g (1$^{1}/_{4}$ lb), cut into pieces

Rempah

Peppercorns	1 tsp
Coriander seeds	2 tsp, roasted
Galangal	14 slices, peeled
Turmeric	$^{1}/_{2}$ Tbsp, peeled
Candlenuts	5, crushed
Shallots	14, peeled
Garlic	1 clove, peeled
Red chillies	2
Shrimp paste (*belacan*)	2 Tbsp

Seasoning

Salt	$^{1}/_{2}$ Tbsp
Sugar	1 tsp
MSG	$^{1}/_{2}$ tsp, optional

METHOD

- Pound *rempah* ingredients together in the given order to make a fine paste.
- Use a piece of muslin to squeeze grated coconut for No.1 milk. Collect in a bowl and set aside.
- Add the water to the grated coconut and squeeze again for No.2 milk. Collect in a separate bowl and set aside.
- In a very hot wok, heat cooking oil. Stir-fry *rempah* paste and bruised lemon grass over moderate heat until fragrant and oil bubbles through.
- Add seasoning ingredients and half of the No.2 milk. When mixture boils, add the bamboo shoots, chicken and pork ribs. Cook for 10 minutes, stirring occasionally.
- Add remaining No.2 milk, stir and cover. Cook over low heat for 20 minutes or until chicken is tender.
- Finally, add No.1 milk. Stir for 1 minute, transfer to a bowl and serve.

Spicy Sambal Kangkung

INGREDIENTS

Red chillies	3, pounded
Shrimp paste (*belacan*)	1 Tbsp
Water convolvulus	
(*kangkung*)	455 g (1 lb)
Cooking oil	4 Tbsp
Sugar	2 tsp
Salt	A pinch
Dried prawns	2 tsp, soaked to soften and pounded

METHOD

- Combine chillies and shrimp paste and pound to a fine paste.
- Discard the tough stalks and roots of the water convolvulus. Cut the vegetable into 7.5-cm (3-in) lengths, wash thoroughly and drain.
- Add 3 Tbsp cooking oil to a heated wok and fry the chilli paste briefly. Add the water convolvulus, sugar, salt and dried prawns.
- Stir-fry over high heat for 1 minute.
- Add the remaining oil, stir well and transfer to a serving plate. Serve hot.

Sambal Belimbing

INGREDIENTS

Bilimbi fruit (*belimbing asam* or *belimbing buluh*)	455 g (1 lb), thinly sliced into rounds
Salt	2 level tsp
Coconut	455 g (1 lb), grated
Cooking oil for frying	
Shallots	115 g (4 oz), peeled and thinly sliced
Garlic	55 g (2 oz), peeled and thinly sliced
Red chillies	4, thinly sliced slantwise
Green chillies	4, thinly sliced slantwise
Water	4 Tbsp
Prawns	455 g (1 lb), shelled and cleaned

Rempah

Shrimp paste (*belacan*)	1 tsp
Candlenuts	2, crushed
Lemon grass	1 stalk, thinly sliced

Seasoning

Salt	1 tsp
Sugar	1/2 tsp
MSG	1/2 tsp, optional

METHOD

- Rub salt into bilimbi fruit and leave to marinate for 1 hour. Rinse, squeeze lightly and set aside.
- Use a piece of muslin and squeeze the coconut to extract about 225 ml (1 cup) of No.1 milk. Set aside.
- Combine *rempah* ingredients and pound into a fine paste.
- Heat cooking oil in a wok. Fry shallots, garlic, red and green chillies separately until light brown. Set aside.
- In a clean wok, heat 4 Tbsp of cooking oil and fry *rempah* paste until fragrant.
- Add the fruit and half the No.1 milk with 4 Tbsp water. Cook for 10 minutes over low heat.
- Add seasoning and prawns and cook until prawns change colour. Stir in remainder of No.1 milk.

Fried Bean Curd with Prawn and
Minced Pork Nyonya Style

INGREDIENTS

Prawns	285 g (10 oz)
Water	285 ml (1 1/4 cups)
Firm bean curd (*taukwa*)	2 pieces, thickly sliced
Yellow bean paste (*taucheo*)	1 Tbsp, pounded
Sugar	1 tsp
Frozen *rempah titik*	55 g (2 oz) (*recipe on page 160*)
Minced pork	115 g (4 oz)

Seasoning

Salt	1/2 tsp
MSG	1/2 tsp, optional
Sugar	1/2 tsp
Pepper	A pinch
Spring onions	2, cut into 4-cm (1 1/2-in) lengths

METHOD

- Shell and devein prawns. Put prawns aside. Wash shells and drain.
- Pound shells coarsely and place in a bowl with 285 ml (1 1/4 cups) water. Strain and set aside stock.
- Place bean curd slices in a bowl of water mixed with a dash of salt and soak for 5 minutes. Drain well.
- Heat 2–3 Tbsp cooking oil in a frying pan and fry the bean curd slices until light brown on both sides. Transfer to a plate.
- Leaving the oil in the pan, increase heat to high and add yellow bean paste, sugar and the *rempah titik* paste. Fry for a minute.
- Add pork and prawns and stir-fry until prawns turn pink. Add prawn stock, seasoning ingredients and fried bean curd slices and cook over moderate heat for 5 minutes.
- Add spring onions, stir, and transfer to a serving plate. Serve hot.

Note:
Grey-shelled prawns give a better fragrance and sweetness to the stock.

Penang Acar

MIXED VEGETABLE PICKLE PENANG STYLE

INGREDIENTS

Cucumber	3.7 kg (8^1/$_4$ lb)
Salt	140 g (5 oz)
Green chillies	20
Red chillies	20
Lime paste	1 tsp (*see note below*)
Cooking oil	570 ml (2^1/$_2$ cups)
Ginger	1 Tbsp, peeled and thinly shredded
Cauliflower	800 g (1^3/$_4$ lb), cut into florettes
Carrots	2, skinned and cut into strips
Cabbage	930 g (2 lb), diced
Peanuts	455 g (1 lb), roasted and pounded
Sesame seeds	8 Tbsp, roasted

Rempah

Shallots	300 g (11 oz), peeled
Turmeric	55 g (2 oz), peeled
Dried chillies	30–40, or 6–8 Tbsp dried chilli paste (*recipe on page 13*)
Red chillies	5

Vinegar Mix A

Rice vinegar	570 ml (2^1/$_2$ cups)
Water	570 ml (2^1/$_2$ cups)
Sugar	455 g (1 lb)
Salt	4 Tbsp

Vinegar Mix B

Water	900 ml (4 cups)
Vinegar	900 ml (4 cups)
Sugar	2 Tbsp
Salt	1 Tbsp

METHOD

- Cut off the ends of the cucumbers. Halve each cucumber lengthwise, then cut each half into two or three pieces again lengthwise. Discard the seeds and pulp.
- Cut cucumber into 5-cm (2-in) lengths. Make a slit halfway down each piece.
- Place the cucumber in a bowl, sprinkle with salt, mix and leave to season for 4–5 hours. Rinse and drain. Place cucumber in a piece of muslin and squeeze out excess water. Set aside.
- Slit the centre of the chillies to remove the seeds. Mix the lime paste in a bowl of water and soak the chillies in it for for 2–3 hours. Drain. (Do not wash the chillies after soaking in lime water.)
- Fill chillies with stuffing (*recipe on page 119*).
- Pound *rempah* ingredients into a fine paste.
- In a heated wok, add cooking oil and heat. Add the shredded ginger and fry until light brown.
- Add the *rempah* paste and stir-fry until fragrant and oil separates. Remove and set aside.
- Add vinegar mix A and bring to the boil for a minute and transfer to a bowl to cool completely.
- In another saucepan, combine vinegar mix B and bring to a rapid boil. Blanch the cucumbers, cauliflower, carrots and cabbage in it separately. Spread out to cool on large trays. (Bring the vinegar water back to a rapid boil each time to blanch the vegetables. Spread the vegetables to cool to keep them crunchy.)
- Heat a wok until very hot. Stir-fry the vegetables separately for 2 minutes with a little oil from the vinegar mixture. Transfer onto trays to cool.
- To mix the pickle: Place the vegetables, *rempah* paste, pounded peanuts and sesame seeds in a large mixing bowl. Mix well and add the stuffed chillies. Leave overnight. Store in dry, clean bottles.

Note:
Lime paste refers to the white chalky edible lime that is used for betelnut chewing. It can be bought at any Indian grocer. The crispness of the chillies can only be achieved by soaking them in 'lime' water.

Stuffing for Chilli

INGREDIENTS

Candlenut	5
Shallots	10, peeled
Shrimp paste (*belacan*)	1 tsp
Cooking oil	225 ml (1 cup)
Salt	1/4 tsp
Sugar	2 Tbsp
Dried prawns	225 g (8 oz), finely pounded
Green papaya	1, medium-sized, skinned, finely grated and dried in the sun (optional)

METHOD

- Pound together the candlenuts, shallots and shrimp paste.
- In a heated frying pan, add cooking oil and pounded paste and fry until fragrant.
- Stir in the salt and sugar.
- Add dried prawns and papaya, if using, and stir until well mixed. Fry over low heat for 5 minutes.
- Cool in a tray before stuffing the chilli.

Acar Timun

CUCUMBER PICKLE

INGREDIENTS

Salt	1¼ tsp
Cucumbers	3, skinned and thinly sliced into rounds
Onions	2, about 115 g (4 oz), peeled and sliced
Red chillies	2, cut lengthwise, seeded and thinly sliced

Seasoning

Salt	1 tsp
Sugar	4 Tbsp
Vinegar	4 Tbsp
Water	2 Tbsp

METHOD

- Combine seasoning ingredients in an enamel saucepan and boil for 2 minutes. Leave to cool.
- Rub 1 tsp salt evenly into cucumber and leave to stand for 10 minutes. Rinse and drain. Set aside.
- Rub the remaining ¼ tsp salt into onions and leave to stand for 10 minutes. Rinse then drain.
- In a bowl, combine all the ingredients including the boiled seasoning, toss and serve.

Spicy Fried Brinjals

INGREDIENTS

Green brinjals	8
Red chillies	15, seeded
Ground cumin	1 tsp
Sugar	1 tsp
Cooking oil	8 Tbsp
Water	2 Tbsp

Seasoning

Salt	1 tsp
MSG	$^1/_2$ tsp, optional
Sugar	1 tsp
Lime juice	1 tsp

METHOD

- Halve brinjals lengthwise and soak in water with some salt for about 15 minutes. Drain.
- Combine chillies, cumin and sugar and pound.
- Heat 6 Tbsp cooking oil in a frying pan and fry brinjals until cooked. Transfer to a large serving plate.
- Leave oil in the pan and add the remaining 2 Tbsp oil. Fry the chilli paste over moderately low heat for 1 minute. Add seasoning ingredients and stir.
- Leave to cook until oil seeps through. Add water, stir and remove from heat.
- Pour *sambal* and oil over brinjals and serve.

Sayur Nangka Masak Lemak

JACKFRUIT AND CHICKEN IN RICH SPICY COCONUT GRAVY

INGREDIENTS

Young jackfruit	680 g (1^1/$_2$ lb), skinned, cut into small pieces
Salt	1 Tbsp
Coconut	560 g (1^1/$_4$ lb), grated
Water	560 ml (2^1/$_2$ cups)
Coriander seeds	1 Tbsp, roasted and finely pounded
Cooking oil	4 Tbsp
Whole chicken	680 g (1^1/$_2$ lb), cut into small pieces
Turmeric leaf (*daun kunyit*)	1
Kaffir lime leaves (*daun limau purut*)	6

Rempah

Shallots or onions	115 g (4 oz), peeled
Garlic	2 cloves, peeled
Candlenuts	2, crushed
Galangal	6 pieces, peeled and thinly sliced
Lemon grass	1 stalk, thinly sliced
Dried chillies	10
Shrimp paste (*belacan*)	1 tsp
Ginger	1 Tbsp, peeled
Turmeric	^{1}/$_2$ Tbsp, peeled, or ^{3}/$_4$ tsp ground turmeric

Seasoning

Sugar	2 tsp
Salt	2 tsp
MSG	1 tsp, optional
Pepper	^{1}/$_2$ tsp

METHOD

- Combine *rempah* ingredients and pound to a fine paste.
- In a saucepan, combine jackfruit and 1 Tbsp salt and enough water to cover the jackfruit. Bring to boil for 20–25 minutes or until jackfruit is tender. Drain jackfruit and set aside.
- Using a piece of muslin, squeeze grated coconut to extract No.1 milk. Collect in a bowl and set aside. Add the 560 ml (2^1/$_2$ cups) water to coconut and squeeze again for No.2 milk. Collect separately and set aside.
- In a frying pan, roast the coriander seeds until fragrant. Pound finely while still hot and set aside.
- Heat 4 Tbsp cooking oil in wok and fry the *rempah* paste over moderate heat for 2 minutes. Add roasted coriander, chicken, seasoning and a quarter of the No.1 milk. Keep stirring for 2 minutes until fragrant and oil separates.
- Add turmeric and kaffir lime leaves, No.2 milk and jackfruit. Cook over moderate heat for ^{1}/$_2$ hour or until chicken is tender.
- Pour in the remaining No.1 milk. Stir well, reduce heat and simmer for 5–7 minutes. Serve.

rice&noodles

NYONYA SPECIALTIES – THE BEST OF SINGAPORE'S RECIPES

Nasi Kuning

YELLOW RICE

INGREDIENTS

Cooking oil	2 Tbsp
Ginger	1 tsp, peeled and pounded
Garlic	4 cloves, peeled
Shallots	6, peeled and thinly sliced
Cinnamon quill	8-cm (3-in) piece
Cardamoms	8, lightly bruised
Cloves	8
Ghee or butter	115 g (4 oz)
Ground turmeric	$1/2$ tsp, blended with 1 Tbsp lime juice
Basmati rice	625 g (1 lb 6 oz), washed and drained
Water	1 litre ($4^1/2$ cups), boiling

Seasoning

MSG	1 tsp, optional
Salt	1 rounded tsp
Chicken stock cube	1

Garnish

Almonds	55 g (2 oz), chopped
Sultanas	115 g (4 oz)

METHOD

- Place cooking oil in a heated wok and heat. Add ginger and fry until brown, followed by garlic and shallots.
- Add the cinnamon quill, cardamoms and cloves and stir-fry.
- Add ghee or butter, and turmeric-lime juice mixture.
- Add the rice and stir-fry until liquid is absorbed.
- Transfer the rice to a saucepan or an electric rice cooker. Pour in the boiling water and add seasoning ingredients. Cook.
- If using a saucepan: Boil with the saucepan covered, or over moderate heat until the rice has absorbed all the water. Reduce the heat and cook for about 15 minutes.
- While rice is cooking, fry the almonds and sultanas. Place 3 Tbsp cooking oil in a heated pan and stir-fry almonds over low heat. When almonds are light brown, remove and drain on absorbent paper. Store in a bottle.
- In the same oil, fry the sultanas for 2 minutes. Drain and cool on absorbent paper.
- When rice is cooked, spoon onto a large platter. Garnish with fried almonds and sultanas and serve.

Birthday Noodles Nyonya Style

INGREDIENTS

Belly pork	285 g (10 oz)
Water	1 litre (4¹/₂ cups)
MSG	1 tsp, optional
Prawns	285 g (10 oz), shelled and deveined (keep shells)
Salt	¹/₄ tsp
Sugar	¹/₄ tsp
Cooking oil	2 Tbsp
Water	1 litre (4¹/₂ cups)

For Prawn-Fish Balls

Prawns	285 g (10 oz), shelled, deveined and finely minced (keep shells)
Fish paste (ready-to-use)	175 g (6 oz)
Salt	³/₄ tsp
MSG	1 tsp, optional
Tapioca flour	1 Tbsp
Red food colouring	2–3 drops
Water	3 Tbsp

For the Noodles

Fine wheat vermicelli (*mee suah*)	225 g (8 oz)
Cooking oil	1 litre (4¹/₂ cups)
Lard	5 Tbsp
Garlic	1 Tbsp, peeled and pounded
Sugar	1 Tbsp
Yellow bean paste (*taucheo*)	1 Tbsp, pounded
Water	450 ml (2 cups)

Garnish

Chinese parsley (coriander leaves	30 g (1 oz), cut into short lengths
Spring onions	30 g (1 oz), cut into 1-cm (¹/₂ -in) lengths
Crisp-fried shallots	3 Tbsp (*recipe on page 12*)

METHOD

- Boil belly pork in 1 litre (4¹/₂ cups) water and 1 tsp MSG, if using. When done, set aside the stock for use later. Slice belly pork into thin strips and set aside.
- Marinate whole prawns with ¹/₄ tsp each of salt and sugar. Set aside.
- In a wok, fry all the prawn shells in 2 Tbsp cooking oil until well cooked. Transfer prawn shells into a saucepan, add 1 litre (4¹/₂ cups) water and boil for 20 minutes. Strain stock and set aside.
- Now make the prawn-fish balls. Combine minced prawns, fish paste salt, MSG, if using, tapioca flour and red food colouring in a large bowl. Roll paste with the palm of your hand in a circular motion to blend. Sprinkle 3 Tbsp water and mix again until paste becomes sticky. Take fistfuls and throw against the side of the bowl (10–15 times) to smoothen paste. Take fistfuls of paste and squeeze through thumb and index finger to make balls, then leave in cold water for ¹/₂ hour.
- Pour prawn and pork stock into a saucepan and bring to a boil. Drop in the prawn-fish balls and let it cook until the balls float. Scoop out and set aside. Keep the stock.

To cook noodles

- Loosen fine wheat vermicelli. Heat 1 litre (4¹/₂ cups) cooking oil in a wok until hot. (Oil is ready when a piece of noodle put in for testing rises to the surface.) Deep-fry each skein of noodles separately until light brown, turning once. Transfer to a plate.
- Pour off the oil from the wok and add in lard. When lard is hot, add garlic and fry until light brown. Add the sugar and yellow bean paste, and stir-fry until oil seeps through. Add 450 ml (2 cups) of the reserved stock, whole prawns, shredded pork and prawn-fish balls. Cook for 2 minutes then remove prawns, pork and prawn-fish balls, leaving behind the gravy.
- Pour in remaining stock and bring to a boil. Reduce heat to low, put in fried vermicelli and stir. When vermicelli softens, season to taste.

- Dish vermicelli onto a large serving plate. Return the prawns, pork and prawn-fish balls to the wok and boil gently in the gravy. When ready, pour gravy over vermicelli. Sprinkle with pepper and garnish. Serve immediately.

Note:
This is a traditional Nyonya dish served only on birthdays. Instead of making tiny prawn-fish balls, the mixture can be made into square patties and boiled in the prawn stock. When cool, cut into small cubes.

The best fine wheat vermicelli is made in China. They are available in boxes and are packed in skeins tied with red string. No seasoning has to be added to the gravy because the vermicelli is quite salty. Season gravy to taste only after vermicelli has been added.

This dish can be served together with Nyonya Salad (*recipe on page 108*).

Nyonya Mahmee

INGREDIENTS

Lard or cooking oil	4 Tbsp
Garlic	1 Tbsp, peeled and pounded
Water convolvulus (*kangkung*)	170 g (6 oz), cut into short lengths
Bean sprouts	625 g (1 lb 6 oz), picked and washed
Fresh yellow egg noodles	625 g (1 lb 6 oz)

For Pork

Streaky pork	170 g (6 oz)
Water	455 ml (2 cups)
Salt	1/4 tsp

For Prawns Stock

Prawns	300 g (11 oz), shelled (keep shells)
Water	455 ml (2 cups)

Seasoning

Yellow bean paste (*taucheo*)	1 Tbsp, pounded
Salt	1/2 tsp
MSG	1 tsp, optional
Pepper	1/2 tsp
Sugar	1 tsp

Garnishing

Cucumber	1, skinned, seeded and finely shredded into 4-cm (1 1/2-in) lengths
Eggs	2, fried into thin omelettes and finely shredded
Crisp-fried shallots	3 Tbsp (*recipe on page 12*)
Red chillies	3, seeded and shredded lengthwise into 4-cm (1 1/2-in) lengths
Pepper	A pinch
Chinese parsley (coriander leaves	1 sprig

METHOD

- **Prepare pork:** Boil the streaky pork in the water with 1/4 tsp salt for 20 minutes. Set aside the stock and slice the boiled pork into thin strips.
- **Prepare prawn stock:** Wash and drain prawn shells. Pound coarsely. Add 455 ml (2 cups) water, stir and strain into a bowl. Set aside.
- Heat lard or cooking oil in a wok and fry pounded garlic until light brown. Add seasoning ingredients and fry for 1 minute.
- Add in the prawn and pork stock and bring to a boil. Add prawns and streaky pork and cook for 1 minute.
- Add water convolvulus, bean sprouts and noodles. Stir-fry for 2–3 minutes over high heat to cook the noodles.
- Dish onto to a large plate and add garnishing. Serve hot.

Laksa Lemak

INGREDIENTS

Cooking oil	225 ml (1 cup)
Lemon grass	2 stalks, bruised
Bean sprouts	625 g (1 lb 6 oz), picked, boiled and drained
Coarse rice vermicelli (*bee hoon*)	1.2 kg (2 lb 11 oz)

Rempah

Turmeric	1 Tbsp, peeled
Galangal	1/2 teacup, peeled and sliced
Dried chillies	20
Red chillies	5
Candlenuts	6, crushed
Shrimp paste (*belacan*)	2 Tbsp
Shallots	225 g (8 oz), peeled
Ground coriander or seeds	1 Tbsp

Coconut Milk

Coconut	1.2 kg (2 lb 11 oz), grated
Water	2.7 litres (12 cups)

For Prawns

Water	455 ml (2 cups)
Salt	1 tsp
Sugar	1 tsp
Prawns	445 g (1 lb)

Seasoning

Dried prawns	55 g (2 oz), pounded
Sugar	1 Tbsp
Salt	2 Tbsp

Garnish

Fish cake	8 pieces, fried and sliced into thin strips
Cucumbers	3, skinned, seeded and sliced lengthwise
Polygonum leaves (*laksa leaves* or *daun kesum*)	55 g (2 oz), finely sliced

METHOD

- Grind *rempah* ingredients to a fine paste.
- Using a piece of muslin, squeeze grated coconut for No.1 milk and collect in a bowl. Add 2.7 litres (12 cups) water to grated coconut and squeeze again to extract No.2 milk. Collect in a separate container and set aside.
- To prepare prawns: Boil the 455 ml (2 cups) water in a saucepan with salt and sugar. Add the prawns and cook for about 5–7 minutes. Remove prawns, shell and slice lengthwise. Set aside.
- Return shells to saucepan, boil for 10 minutes and strain liquid for stock.
- To prepare gravy: Heat cooking oil in a wok and fry *rempah* paste and lemon grass until fragrant and the oil separates.
- Add No.2 milk and prawn stock and bring to a boil. Add seasoning ingredients and boil for 10 minutes over low heat.
- Reduce the heat and simmer. Add No.1 milk, setting aside 2 Tbsp for the chilli paste (*recipe on page 135*). Stir for a minute then remove from heat. Continue stirring to prevent curdling.
- Serve in individual portions. Place some bean sprouts and rice vermicelli in bowls. Add hot gravy and garnish with prepared prawns, fish cake, cucumber, polygonum leaves and chilli paste (*recipe on page 135*).

Note:
Cellophane noodles (*tang hoon*) can also be added to the rice vermicelli.

This recipe serves 10.

Chili Paste

INGREDIENTS

Dried chillies	55 g (2 oz)
Red chillies	5
Shrimp paste *(belacan)*	1 tsp
Cooking oil	2 Tbsp
Water	1–2 Tbsp
Sugar	2 tsp
Salt	1 tsp
No.1 coconut milk	2 Tbsp *(reserved from main recipe on page 134)*

METHOD

- Combine red and dried chillies and shrimp paste and grind to a fine paste.
- Heat pan until hot. Heat cooking oil and fry chili paste until well done and oil comes through.
- Add 1–2 Tbsp water, salt, sugar and No.1 coconut milk and fry.
- Transfer to a bowl.

nyonyakuih
NYONYA SPECIALTIES – THE BEST OF SINGAPORE'S RECIPES

Kuih Bangkit

INGREDIENTS

Rice flour	225 g (8 oz)
Tapioca flour	455 g (1 lb)
Coconut	455 g (1 lb), skinned and grated
Eggs	5
Sugar	400 g (14 oz)
Salt	$^3/_4$ tsp

METHOD

- Place rice flour in a dry wok and stir over low heat until very light and fluffy. Remove rice flour and set aside. Repeat with tapioca flour.
- Combine the two flours and sift together in a basin. Leave overnight.
- Using a piece of muslin, squeeze coconut to extract No.1 milk. Set aside. You should get 225 ml (1 cup).
- In a mixing bowl, combine eggs and sugar and beat until thick and creamy. Add salt and coconut milk and beat until well blended.
- Set aside 115 g (4 oz) of the sifted flour for dusting.
- Set aside 200 ml ($^3/_4$ cup) of the egg mixture.
- Mix the remaining egg mixture into the flour to form a dough. Take a handful of the dough and place it on a dusted board. Keep the rest of the dough covered with a damp cloth.
- Flatten the dough with palm of hand. Dust with flour and roll dough out to 0.5-cm ($^1/_4$-in) thickness.
- Cut dough with a *kuih bangkit* cutter (*see picture on the left*). Pinch the dough, using a jagged-edged pincers (usually used for pineapple tarts) to form a pattern.
- Mix leftover dough cuttings with another lot of new dough and a little of the beaten egg mixture each time. Mix dough to a smooth texture before rolling out and repeating process.
- Place biscuits on greased baking trays and bake in an oven for 20–30 minutes at 175°C (350°F). Cool biscuits on a rack before storing in an airtight tin.

Kuih Bolu

NYONYA SPONGE SMALL CAKE

INGREDIENTS

Plain flour	170 g (6 oz)
Baking powder	1 1/2 tsp
Eggs	5
Castor sugar	155 g (5 oz)

METHOD

- Preheat oven to 200°C (400°F).
- Combine flour and baking powder and sift twice. Divide into two equal portions and set aside.
- In a mixing bowl, combine eggs and sugar and beat until thick and creamy. Divide into two portions.
- Sift one portion of the flour over one portion of the egg mixture. Fold flour into the egg mixture very lightly.
- Grease and heat *kuih bolu* pans (*see picture on the left*). Spoon batter into the pans until three-quarter full. Bake in the oven for 5 minutes, then reduce the temperature to 150°C (300°F). Continue baking until cake turns golden brown.
- When done, transfer to cool on a rack.
- Repeat with remaining egg and flour. Wait until oven temperature reaches 200°C (400°F) again before baking. Bake at once when batter is spooned into the moulds. Do not leave to stand.
- Cool cakes completely and store in an airtight containers.

Kuih Lompang

STEAMED RICE CAKES WITH COCONUT TOPPING

INGREDIENTS

Rice flour	140 g (5 oz)
Water	500 ml (about 2 1/4 cups)
Tapioca flour	1 heaped Tbsp
Coarse sugar	285 g (10 oz)
Screwpine (*pandan*) leaves	8, knotted
Food colouring	A variety
Coconut	455 g (1 lb), coarsely grated and mixed with a pinch of salt

METHOD

- Mix the rice and tapioca flour in 75 ml (1/3 cup) water. Stir well.
- In a pan, boil sugar and screwpine leaves in the remaining 425 ml (1 3/4 cups) water for 5 minutes or until sugar dissolves.
- Pour the syrup gradually through a strainer into the flour mixture, stirring constantly.
- Divide the mixture into 3 or 4 portions. Put one or two drops of food colouring into each portion to make light pastel shades. (The colour deepens on steaming, so use colour sparingly).
- Place small Chinese teacups (*see picture on the left*) in a steamer over rapidly boiling water to heat for 5 minutes. Fill cups with coloured flour mixture and steam for 10 minutes. Wipe condensation off lid after 5 minutes' steaming.
- Remove cups and allow cakes to cool for about 20 minutes.
- Remove cakes from cups with a blunt knife, roll the cakes in the grated coconut and serve.

Note:
To facilitate filling of small cups, pour mixture from a teapot. Stir mixture well for an even consistency.

Kuih Ko Chee

STEAMED GLUTINOUS RICE PASTE WITH COCONUT FILLING

INGREDIENTS

Banana leaves	20, 20 cm (8 in) in diameter
Coconut	455 g (1 lb), skinned and grated
Water	115 ml (1/2 cup)
Sweet potato	115 g (4 oz), skinned
Glutinous rice flour	400 g (14 oz)
Salt	A pinch
Sugar	2 Tbsp
Cooking oil	2 Tbsp
Blue food colouring	2 drops

METHOD

- Wipe banana leaves with a wet cloth and scald in a saucepan of boiling water for 1 minute. Drain.
- Place grated coconut in a piece of muslin and squeeze to extract 200 ml (about 1 cup) No.1 milk. Collect in a bowl and set aside.
- Add 115 ml (1/2 cup) water to coconut and squeeze again to extract No.2 milk. Collect in a separate bowl and set aside.

- In a saucepan, boil sweet potato gently until cooked, then mash until smooth. Mix well with 225 g (8 oz) of the glutinous rice flour and set aside.
- In another saucepan, combine No.2 milk, salt, sugar and cooking oil and bring to a boil. Add the food colouring, remove from heat and add the remaining flour. Stir lightly. Cool for 1 minute.
- Put the sweet potato mixture in a saucepan, add the No.1 milk and stir with wooden spoon until it forms a paste.
- Add the No.2 milk mixture and knead the paste lightly to form a smooth firm dough. Add a little flour if dough is too soft.
- Divide dough into 4 portions and cut each portion into a further 16 pieces. Roll each piece into a ball, put in a knob of coconut filling (see recipe below) and seal.
- Fold each banana leaf into a cone, put in dough, and fold the top of the banana leaf cone over to form a triangle. Staple the ends to secure.
- Repeat with the rest of the paste and steam over moderately high heat for 15 minutes.

Coconut Filling

INGREDIENTS

Sugar	3 Tbsp
Palm sugar (*gula Melaka*)	285 g (10 oz), grated
Water	3 Tbsp
Screwpine (*pandan*) leaves	6
Coconut	570 g (1 1/4 lb), grated
Pearl sago	1 Tbsp, mixed with 2 Tbsp water

METHOD

- In a wok, combine sugar, palm sugar, water and screwpine leaves. Boil until the sugar turns syrupy.
- Add grated coconut and lower the heat. Stir mixture constantly until almost dry.
- Add the sago mixture, stir thoroughly and cook for another 5 minutes. Remove to a tray to cool.

Note:
A simpler way of wrapping *kuih ko chee* is to put filling in the centre of each piece of dough, roll it into a ball, then place on a piece of softened banana leaf and fold into a neat bundle. Staple the ends and steam. Any leftover filling can be stored in the freezer for future use.

Kuih Bingka Ubi Kayu

NYONYA TAPIOCA CAKE

INGREDIENTS

Tapioca	1.4 kg (3 lb), skinned and finely grated
Cold water	225 ml (1 cup)
Coconut	900 g (2 lb), skinned and grated
Water	170 ml ($^3/_4$ cup)
Castor sugar	480 g (17 oz)
Sago flour or cornflour	3 tsp
Eggs	3, lightly beaten
Butter	1 Tbsp, melted
Vanilla essence	1$^1/_2$ tsp
Salt	1$^1/_2$ level tsp

METHOD

- Preheat oven to 175°C (350°F).
- In a bowl, combine grated tapioca and 225 ml (1 cup) cold water. Place handfuls of grated tapioca in a piece of muslin and squeeze, collecting the tapioca water in a small saucepan.
- Set grated tapioca and the saucepan of tapioca water aside. Allow tapioca water to stand so that the tapioca starch settles at the bottom of pan. After about $^1/_2$ hour, carefully pour water away, leaving the starch in the pan. Mix tapioca starch with grated tapioca.
- Place grated coconut in a piece of muslin and squeeze to extract No.1 milk. Collect 455 ml (2 cups) of the No.1 milk in a bowl and set aside. Add 170 ml ($^3/_4$ cup) water to grated coconut and squeeze again to extract 170 ml ($^3/_4$ cup) of No.2 milk. Collect in a separate bowl and set aside.
- Add the sugar, flour, eggs, butter, vanilla essence and salt to the No.2 milk and whisk lightly until blended. Pour mixture into a saucepan and cook over moderate heat until heated through and sugar dissolves. Add No.1 milk and cook for another minute.
- Put grated tapioca into a large mixing bowl. Pour in the hot egg and coconut mixture and stir until well blended.
- Grease a square baking tin (20 x 20 x 4 cm). Line the sides of the tin with greaseproof paper, allowing 0.5 cm ($^1/_4$ in) clearance from the sides. Grease the paper and dust tin with flour.
- Put tapioca mixture into tin and bake for 10–15 minutes or until cake turns light brown. Reduce heat to 135°C (275°F) and cook for another 1–1$^1/_2$ hours or until cake is golden brown.
- Cool on a rack for 10 minutes. Remove cake from tin and allow to cool completely. Slice and serve.

Seri Kaya

RICH EGG CUSTARD

INGREDIENTS

Coconut	900 g (2 lb), grated
Eggs	10
Sugar	560 g (1¼ lb), coarse
Screwpine (*pandan*) leaves	2, knotted

METHOD

Stirring method

• Place grated coconut in a piece of muslin and squeeze to extract 400 ml (1½ cups) No.1 milk. Collect in a container and set aside.

• In another bowl, beat eggs and sugar until well mixed.

• Place egg mixture and screwpine leaves in an enamel bowl over a very low heat and stir to dissolve the sugar. (This takes about 10 minutes.) Stir constantly with a wooden spoon. Remove from heat and discard screwpine leaves.

• Add No.1 milk to the egg mixture, then strain into a double boiler*.

• Place over a low flame and heat egg mixture until it becomes thick like custard cream. This will take about 45 minutes. Stir often.

• Transfer to a bowl or bottle.

Note:
If you don't have a double boiler*, strain the egg mixture into an enamel bowl. Place the bowl on a rack in saucepan or wok of rapidly boiling water and reduce the egg mixture according to the recipe above.

Steaming method

• To steam, follow the recipe up to the point where the No.1 milk is added to the egg mixture. Place mixture into a heat-proof container.

• Wrap lid of container with a dry tea-towel. Place container, with lid on, on a rack in a saucepan or wok.

• Place enough hot water in the saucepan to reach about 2.5 cm (1 in) above the base of the container. Cover saucepan and steam for 3 hours over moderate heat. Do not stir.

• Dry the underside of the cover of the saucepan occasionally to prevent discolouration of the *seri kaya*.

Pinapple 'Open' Tarts

INGREDIENTS

Ice water	55 ml (¹/₄ cup)
Vanilla essence	2 tsp
Egg	1, lightly beaten
Yellow food colouring	3 drops
Plain flour	680 g (1¹/₂ lb)
Salt	1 tsp
Castor sugar	2 Tbsp
Butter	455 g (1 lb)

METHOD

- Combine ice water, vanilla essence, egg and yellow food colouring in a bowl and set aside.
- Sift together flour, salt and sugar.
- Using fingertips, rub butter into flour until mixture resembles breadcrumbs.
- Add egg and vanilla essence mixture to the flour and mix to form a pastry dough. Chill for ¹/₂ hour.
- On a floured board or marble table top, roll pastry to 0.5-cm (¹/₄-in) thick. Cut with a special tart cutter (see inset picture on page 151).

- Fill tarts with pineapple filling (see recipe below).
- Using special brass pincers (see picture below), pinch a small neat frill or pattern around the edge of tart. Cut thin strips from leftover dough to decorate top of the tart.
- Place tarts on a greased baking tray and bake in an oven at 175°C (350°F) for 15 minutes.
- Reduce heat and bake for another 10–15 minutes until light brown.
- Turn tarts out to cool on a wire rack before storing in an airtight container.

Note:
Brass pincers can be found in local provision shops.

Pineapple Filling

INGREDIENTS

Pineapples	6, preferably Mauritian, skinned, 'eyes' removed and coarsely grated
Coarse sugar	(See note)
Cloves	3
Cinnamon quill	5-cm (2-in) length
Star anise	2 petals

METHOD

- Using a piece of muslin, squeeze juice out of the pineapple (but do not squeeze pineapple too dry).
- Wearing clean gloves, chop pineapples until fine.
- In a heavy bottomed pan, combine pineapple pulp, sugar, cloves, cinnamon quill and star anise. Cook over moderate heat until almost dry – about 1 hour.
- Reduce heat to low and continue cooking until mixture is thick. Stir often to prevent pineapple from burning.
- Cool and store overnight in the refrigerator.
- Shape mixture into long cylindrical rolls about 2.5 cm (1 in) in diameter. Cut into 1-cm (¹/₅-in) pieces and shape into balls.
- Place balls on a tray and chill until ready for use.

Note:
The volume of sugar should be exactly the same as that of the pineapple pulp. (ie. 1 cup sugar to 1 cup pineapple pulp.)

Kuih Ko Swee

RICE CUP CAKES

INGREDIENTS

Wet rice flour	285 g (10 oz) (*recipe on page 13*)
Sago flour	285 g (10 oz)
Cold water	570 ml (2¹/₂ cups)
Alkaline water	3 Tbsp (*recipe on page 13*)
Palm sugar (*gula Melaka*)	455g (1 lb)
Sugar	225 g (8 oz), coarse
Screwpine (*pandan*) leaves	10, cut into 5-cm (2-in) lengths
Water	455 ml (2 cups)
Coconut	455 g (1 lb) skinned and grated, mixed with a pinch of fine salt

METHOD

- In a bowl, combine rice flour, sago flour, cold water and alkaline water. Set aside.
- Place the sugars, screwpine leaves and water in a saucepan and bring to boil for 10 minutes. Strain into the flour mixture, stirring with a wooden spoon until well mixed.
- Place small Chinese cups (*see picture on page 142*) in a steamer or on a stand in a wok and steam for 5 minutes to heat. Then fill cups with the flour mixture and steam over a high heat for 7 minutes.
- Cool and remove cake from each cup. Roll cakes in grated coconut and serve.

sambal,pickles&sauces

NYONYA SPECIALTIES – THE BEST OF SINGAPORE'S RECIPES

Sweet Chilli Sauce

INGREDIENTS

Red chillies	455 g (1 lb), washed and drained
Water	1 litres (5 cups)
Sugar	340 g (12 oz), coarse grain
Salt	4 Tbsp
Vinegar	170 ml (³/₄ cup)

Rempah

Dried chilli paste (recipe on page 13)	115 g (4 oz), or 55 g (2 oz) dried chillies
Shrimp paste (belacan)	1 Tbsp
Sultanas	55 g (2 oz)
Ginger	85 g (3 oz), peeled and thinly sliced
Garlic	6 cloves, peeled

METHOD

- Combine *rempah* ingredients with half the red chillies and blend until it becomes a fine paste. Add some water if paste gets too thick.
- Set aside. Blend or pound the remaining red chilli.
- Pour the rest of the water, sugar and salt into a non-stick saucepan and bring to a boil.
- Add the chilli and *rempah* paste and boil over moderate heat for 20 minutes, stirring occasionally to prevent it from burning.
- Lower heat and continue to cook for 1 hour. Stir occasionally until sauce thickens.
- Pour mixture into an enamel saucepan. Add the vinegar and boil for another 10 minutes.
- Leave to cool completely and store in dry bottles.

Note:
Fill each bottle to the top with chilli sauce and screw on the plastic cover tightly before storing. If a metal cap is used, line it with a piece of waxed paper to prevent rust. Store in a cool place or in the refrigerator.

Hot Chilli Sauce

INGREDIENTS

Dried chillies	55 g (2 oz)
Red chillies	625 g (1 lb 6 oz)
Water	285ml (1 cup)
Garlic	8 cloves, peeled
Ginger	1 thumb-sized piece, peeled and sliced
Salt	5 Tbsp
Sugar	455 g (1 lb)
Rice vinegar	170 ml (³/₄ cup)

METHOD

- Put a little water in a pan, add dried chillies and boil for 2 minutes. Turn off the heat and leave to soak for 5 minutes. Remove chillies from the pan and rinse with water until the water runs clear. Place in a colander to drain.
- Put half the chillies in an electric blender together with 285 ml (1 cup) water and blend chillies until very fine. Remove and set aside. Repeat process with the remaining chillies, adding the garlic and ginger.
- In an enamel saucepan, combine the 2 batches of liquidized chilli mixture as well as the water remaining in the blender. Add salt and bring to boil over moderate heat, stirring constantly for 10 minutes.
- Stir in the sugar. Bring chilli sauce to a boil. Lower the heat and simmer for 1¹/₂ hours, stirring occasionally.
- Add the vinegar, stir and continue boiling for 5 minutes.
- Remove from the heat. Cool before storing in dry, clean bottles.

Garam Asam Paste

INGREDIENTS

Galangal	340 g (12 oz), peeled and sliced
Lemon grass	340 g (12 oz) sliced
Shrimp paste (*belacan*)	455 g (1 lb)
Candlenuts	285 g (10 oz), crushed
Red chillies	680 g (1 1/2 lb)
Onions	1.4 kg (3 lb), peeled
Turmeric powder	40 g (1 1/2 oz)
Chilli powder	30 g (1 oz), or dried chilli ground to a fine paste
Cooking oil for frying	710 ml (3 cups)

METHOD

- Blend galangal, lemon grass, shrimp paste and candlenuts to a fine paste.
- Roughly pound chillies and onions separately.
- Combine all the ingredients, except for the cooking oil, and mix until well blended.
- Heat wok until very hot, then add cooking oil. When oil is smoking hot, add in half the spice mixture.
- Fry over moderately high heat until oil bubbles through. Stir constantly to prevent the paste from burning.
- Add the rest of the spice mixture and continue to stir.
- Lower heat and keep frying until paste is fragrant and almost dry.
- Remove and let cool completely before packing into 455 g (1 lb) portions in plastic bags or airtight containers.
- Store in freezer for future use.

Chilli Garam Paste

INGREDIENTS

Red chillies	600 g (1 lb 5 oz)
Shrimp paste (*belacan*)	85 g (3 oz), finely diced
Cooking oil	225 ml (1 cup)
Salt	2 1/2 Tbsp
Sugar	2 Tbsp
Water	85 ml (1/3 cup)

METHOD

- Coarsely pound together chillies and shrimp paste.
- Heat cooking oil in pan, add the chilli paste and fry over moderate heat until fragrant and oil bubbles through.
- Add remaining ingredients and stir-fry until moist and oily.
- Leave to cool completely before packing into plastic containers. Store in freezer for future use.

Note:
When the chilli paste freezes, cut into cubes of 4 cm (1 1/2 in), then put them back into the freezer. You can then thaw the amount you need each time.

Rempah Titik

This is a basic *rempah* for Fried Bean Cake with Prawn and Minced Pork Nyonya Style (*page 116*).

INGREDIENTS

Shallots or onions	680 g (1 1/2 lb), peeled
Dried chillies	20, softened
Garlic	2 cloves, peeled
Candlenuts	8, crushed
Shrimp paste *(belacan)*	55 g (2 oz)
Cooking oil	225 ml (1 cup)

METHOD

- Combine all the ingredients except for the cooking oil, and grind or blend to a fine paste.
- In a hot wok, add cooking oil and heat. When hot, add the paste and fry until fragrant and oil bubbles through. Stir often to prevent the paste from sticking to the bottom of the pan.
- Transfer to a large bowl to cool completely. Pack in plastic containers or bags and freeze for future use.

Dried Chilli Paste

INGREDIENTS

Dried chillies	225 g (8 oz), stems removed
Water	450 ml (1 cup)

METHOD

- Place chillies in a saucepan, three-quarter filled with cold water.
- Bring to a boil and cook for 5 minutes. Cover pan and leave chillies to soak for 10 minutes. Drain.
- Place chilli in a large basin and wash until water runs clear. Drain.
- Using an electric blender, blend half of the chillies with 225 ml (1 cup) water until very fine. Remove paste and repeat process with the other half of the chillies and water.
- Store chilli paste in a plastic container. Keep in freezer until needed.

Note:
Keep chilli paste rotating while blending. Add a little water if paste is not rotating. Makes about 32 Tbsp of chilli paste.

Sambal Tumis

BASIC SAMBAL

INGREDIENTS

Coconut	115 g (4 oz), grated
Water	55 ml (¹/₄ cup)
Cooking oil	6 Tbsp

Rempah

Shallots	15, peeled
Dried chillies	30, or 3 Tbsp dried chilli paste (*recipe on page 13*)
Shrimp paste (*belacan*)	1 Tbsp
Garlic	1 clove, peeled

Seasoning

Sugar	1 tsp
Salt	¹/₂ tsp
MSG	A pinch, optional
Tamarind pulp (*asam*)	1 Tbsp, mixed with 55 ml (¹/₄ cup) water, squeezed and strained

METHOD

- Combine *rempah* ingredients and pound to a fine paste.
- Combine grated coconut with 55 ml (¹/₄ cup) water. Place in a piece of muslin and squeeze to extract No.2 coconut milk. Collect in a bowl and set aside.
- Heat cooking oil in a wok and fry *rempah* paste over moderate heat until oil bubbles through.
- Add half the coconut milk and stir for about 2 minutes. Add seasoning ingredients, cover and cook for another 2 minutes.
- Add the rest of the coconut milk, stir for one minute and serve.

Salted Fish Sambal

INGREDIENTS

Penang salted fish	140 g (5 oz), thinly sliced
Cooking oil	170 ml (³/₄ cup)
Garlic	6 cloves, peeled
Shallots	4, peeled
Shrimp paste (*belacan*)	1 tsp
Red chillies	5, seeded
Tomatoes	2, thinly sliced
Red bird's eye chillies (*cili padi*)	10, stems removed and lightly bruised
Green bird's eye chillies (*cili padi*)	10, stems removed and lightly bruised
Water	4 Tbsp

Seasoning

Sugar	2 tsp
MSG	¹/₂ tsp, optional
Vinegar	1 tsp

METHOD

- Soak salted fish in cold water for 1 minute. Drain for 10 minutes.
- Heat cooking oil in a pan. Put in salted fish and fry until pale brown. Place fish in a wire sieve to drain and cool (about 5 minutes).
- Reheat the oil until very hot. Return fish to the pan and stir-fry for 2–3 minutes until light golden brown. Place fish on absorbent paper and cool. Set aside in a container.
- Reserve oil for frying *sambal*.
- Coarsely pound garlic, shallots, shrimp paste and red chillies.
- In a pan, heat 3 Tbsp of the reserved oil. Add the pounded mixture and stir-fry until fragrant and lightly brown. Add sliced tomatoes and bird's eye chillies and fry until oil bubbles through. Add the water and seasoning ingredients and cook over moderate heat until mixture is thick and oily.
- Add in salted fish and stir to mix thoroughly just before serving.

Note:
Both fried fish and *sambal* can be prepared ahead and stored. To serve, reheat *sambal* and add salted fish.

Sambal for Crispy Anchovies

INGREDIENTS

Dried chillies	115 g (4 oz), washed
Garlic	1 clove, peeled
Shallots or onions	115 g (4 oz), peeled
Shrimp paste *(belacan)*	55 g (2 oz)
Coconut	170 g (6 oz), grated
Water	225 ml (1 cup)
Cooking oil	170 ml ($^3/_4$ cup)

Seasoning

Sugar	4 level tbsp
Salt	$^1/_4$ tsp
MSG	1 tsp, optional
Tamarind pulp *(asam)*	1 Tbsp, mixed with 4 Tbsp water, squeezed and strained

METHOD

- Soak dried chillies in water to soften. Combined softened chillies with garlic, shallots and shrimp paste and pound to a fine paste.
- Combine coconut with the water. Using a piece of muslin, squeeze coconut to extract No.2 coconut milk. Set aside.
- Add cooking oil to a heated wok. When oil is hot, fry chilli paste and one-third of the milk over moderate heat until fragrant and oil bubbles through.
- Stir in seasoning ingredients and the remaining coconut milk. Lower heat and simmer for 2 minutes. Remove to a bowl to cool.
- Divide into four portions, pack in plastic bags and freeze for future use.

Note:
Each portion can be mixed with 170 g (16 oz) crispy anchovies and served as a side dish for Nasi Lemak.

To fry anchovies to a crisp

- Remove heads of medium-sized anchovies. Wash and drain the anchovies.
- Heat cooking oil for deep-frying until very hot. Add the anchovies and fry over moderate heat until crisp and light brown. Lower heat at the end of cooking time to prevent it from turning too dark.
- Remove anchovies to cool slightly on a paper towel and store in a container.
- Thaw a portion of the *sambal*, heat through in a frying pan. Combine *sambal* with the crispy anchovies when ready to serve.

Sambal Belacan

INGREDIENTS

Kaffir lime leaves (*daun limau purut*)	4, optional
Red chillies	225 g (8 oz)
Shrimp paste (*belacan*)	115 g (4 oz), toasted and broken into small pieces
Salt	2 level tsp
Sugar	2 level tsp

METHOD

- Remove central vein of lime leaves, shred finely, then pound until very fine.
- Remove stems from chillies and dip in water. Place wet chillies in blender, add toasted shrimp paste, salt and sugar and blend well. Remove from blender. Mix with the pounded lime leaves.
- Pack into plastic containers and freeze.

Note:
The slender variety of chilli is more fragrant and tastes better.

If using a pestle and mortar, pound the lime leaves until very fine, then add the chillies, salt, sugar and shrimp paste. Pound until well blended.

Basic Rempah Rendang

(PICTURE ON OPPOSITE PAGE: LEFT)

INGREDIENTS

Onions	1.4 kg (3 lb)
Lemon grass	225 g (8 oz), sliced
Galangal	225 g (8 oz), peeled and sliced
Candlenuts	170 g (6 oz), crushed
Ginger	115 g (4 oz), peeled and sliced
Garlic	55 g (2 oz), peeled and sliced
Shrimp paste (*belacan*)	115 g (4 oz)
Curry powder	115 g (4 oz)
Chilli powder	55 g (2 oz), or dried chilli, ground to a fine paste
Cooking oil	680 ml (3 cups)
Coconut	455 g (1 lb), grated

For Coconut Milk

Coconut	1.4 kg (3 lb), grated
Water	225 ml (1 cup)

METHOD

- Place handfuls of grated coconut in a piece of muslin and squeeze to extract No.1 milk. Collect in a bowl and set aside. Add the water to coconut and squeeze again for No.2 milk. Collect separately and set aside.
- Pound or blend onions, lemon grass, galangal, candlenuts, ginger, garlic and shrimp paste into a fine paste. Set aside.
- Mix the curry powder, chilli powder or paste with the No.2 milk. Then combine with the pounded spice paste. Set aside.
- Heat a wok until very hot. Add 570 ml (2$^{1}/_{2}$ cups) cooking oil and heat until smoking hot. Add the 455 g (1 lb) grated coconut and fry until brown. Transfer the coconut into a metal colander and drain. Set aside the oil. Spread coconut on a large tray to cool, then pound until fine. Set aside.
- Heat wok until very hot. Pour in the oil from frying the coconut and add the remaining 115 ml ($^{1}/_{2}$ cup) oil. Heat until oil smokes. Put in the spice paste and fry until fragrant and oil bubbles through. Add 170 ml ($^{3}/_{4}$ cup) No.1 milk and continue frying until paste is almost dry and oil seeps through to the surface.
- Add the rest of the No.1 milk, reduce heat, then add pounded fried coconut. Cook for another 5–10 minutes, stirring often until paste is almost dry.
- Remove to a large tray to cool completely. Pack 455 g (1 lb) portions in plastic bags or containers and freeze for future use.

Rempah Gulai

(PICTURE ON PAGE 169: LEFT)

INGREDIENTS

Candlenuts	10
Lemon grass	115 g (4 oz), sliced
Dried chillies	115 g (4 oz), softened
Onions	1.2 kg (2 lb 6 oz), peeled
Shrimp paste (*belacan*)	85 g (3 oz)
Turmeric powder	4 Tbsp
Cooking oil	225 ml (1 cup)
Water	2 Tbsp
Sugar	10 Tbsp
Salt	1 tsp

METHOD

- Combine candlenuts, lemon grass and dried chillies and pound or blend until fine.
- Add the onions and shrimp paste and blend to a fine paste. Transfer paste to a bowl. Add the turmeric powder and mix well.
- Put cooking oil into a heated wok. When oil is hot, add the spice paste and fry until fragrant and oil bubbles through.
- Add the water, sugar and salt and cook over low heat for 1–2 minutes.
- Transfer paste to a bowl and cool completely.
- Pack in plastic bags and store in freezer for future use.

Rendang Rempah for Seafood

(PICTURE ON PAGE 167: RIGHT)

INGREDIENTS

Coconut	3, grated, or 570 ml ($2^1/_2$ cups) No.1 coconut milk
Cooking oil	850 ml ($3^3/_4$ cups)
Kaffir lime leaves (*daun limau purut*)	30, optional

Rempah

Candlenuts	170 g (6 oz), crushed
Onions	1.2 kg (2 lb 11 oz), peeled
Galangal	285 g (10 oz), peeled and sliced
Lemon grass	285 g (10 oz), sliced
Dried chillies	225 g (8 oz), soaked
Shrimp paste (*belacan*)	170 g (6 oz)
Ginger	85 g (3 oz), peeled and sliced

Seasoning

Curry powder	225 g (8 oz)
Pepper	2 tsp
Turmeric powder	2 Tbsp

METHOD

- Combine *rempah* ingredients and pound or blend into a very fine paste.
- Using a piece of muslin, squeeze grated coconut in batches to extract about 570 ml ($2^1/_2$ cups) No.1 milk. Collect in a bowl.
- In another bowl, combine seasoning ingredients.
- Heat a large wok until very hot. Add half the cooking oil and heat. Add the *rempah* paste and fry until fragrant and oil bubbles through. Stir frequently. Add the rest of the oil and the seasoning, lower heat and stir-fry until fragrant. Stir frequently to prevent paste sticking to the bottom of the pan.
- Now pour in the coconut milk and stir over low heat for 2 minutes.
- Add lime leaves and stir.
- Transfer to a large tray to cool. Pack in plastic bags and freeze.

Curry Rempah

(PICTURE ON OPPOSITE PAGE: RIGHT)

INGREDIENTS

Coconut	900 g (2 lb), grated
Water	455 ml (2 cups)
Curry powder	455 g (1 lb)
Cooking oil	570 ml ($2^1/_2$ cups)
Ginger	225 g (8 oz), peeled and thinly shredded
Garlic	55 g (2 oz), peeled and pounded
Onions	900 g (2 lb), peeled and thinly sliced
Shrimp paste (*belacan*)	85 g (3 oz), mixed to a paste with 115 ml ($1/_2$ cup) water
Water	55 ml ($1/_4$ cup)

METHOD

- For the coconut milk: Place small handfuls of grated coconut in a piece of muslin and squeeze to extract No.1 milk. Set aside.
- Add the 455 ml (2 cups) water to the coconut and squeeze again for No.2 milk. Collect in a separate bowl.
- Add curry powder to No.2 milk and stir to combine.
- Heat a wok until very hot. Heat cooking oil and fry the ginger until very lightly brown. Add garlic and fry until lightly brown. Increase heat, add onions and fry until transparent and slightly brown.
- Add shrimp paste and stir-fry for a minute. Put in the curry and coconut milk mixture and half of the No.1 milk. Lower heat and stir to combine.
- Add the rest of the milk and continue stirring to prevent the paste from sticking to the bottom of the pan.
- When oil bubbles through, add 55 ml ($1/4$ cup) water. Stir for a minute before transferring to a large bowl to cool completely.
- Pack in 455 g (1 lb) packets and store in freezer for future use.

Kurma Powder

INGREDIENTS

Coriander seeds	600 g (1 lb 5 oz)
Cumin seeds	285 g (10 oz)
Aniseeds	225 g (8 oz)
White peppercorns	225 g (8 oz)
Poppy seeds	75 g (2¹/₂ oz), optional

METHOD

- Wash coriander, cumin and aniseeds in separately, drain and spread out to dry in sun.
- Put the white peppercorns on a tray. Heat oven slightly and toast peppercorns for 30–45 minutes until peppercorns are heated through and fragrant.
- Combine all the ingredients and blend in a spice mill. Spread to cool completely and store in airtight containers or sealed plastic bags.

Curry Powder for Meat Curry

INGREDIENTS

Coriander seeds	1.2 kg (2 lb 11 oz)
Cumin seeds	425 g (15 oz)
Aniseeds	285 g (10 oz)
Dried chilli	425 g (15 oz)
Turmeric	140 g (5 oz)
White peppercorns	140 g (5 oz)
Cinnamon bark	75 g (2¹/₂ oz)
Cloves	40
Nutmeg	3
Cardamom	50
Star anise	2
Poppy seeds	75 g (2¹/₂ oz), optional

METHOD

- Wash coriander, cumin and aniseeds separately. Drain well and dry in the sun together with the dried chilli.
- Put the rest of the ingredients on a tray, except for the poppy seeds.
- Heat oven slightly and toast the tray of ingredients for 30–45 minutes until ingredients are heated through and fragrant.
- Mix all the ingredients together and blend in a spice mill.
- Spread to cool completely, then store in airtight bottles or sealed plastic bags.

Rempah Tumis for Fish Curry

INGREDIENTS

Cumin seeds	55 g (2 oz)
Cinnamon bark	55 g (2 oz)
Fenugreek	55 g (2 oz)
Split black beans	55 g (2 oz)
Poppy seeds	30 g (1 oz)

METHOD

- Wash cumin seeds and cinnamon bark. Drain.
- Dry in sun or under a warm grill for 35–45 minutes until ingredients are heated through and smell fragrant.
- Combine all the ingredients and place in a bottle. Store in refrigerator for future use.

Curry Powder for Fish Curry

INGREDIENTS

Coriander seeds	600 g (1 lb 5 oz)
Cumin seeds	140 g (5 oz)
Aniseeds	310 g (11 oz)
Dried chilli	310 g (11 oz)
White peppercorns	75 g (2 1/2 oz)
Black peppercorns	35 g (1 1/4 oz)
Dried turmeric	115 g (4 oz)

METHOD

- Wash coriander, cumin and aniseeds separately, drain and dry in the sun together with the dried chillies.
- Put the rest of the ingredients on a tray. Heat oven slightly and toast ingredients for 30–45 minutes until ingredients are heated through and fragrant.
- Mix all the ingredients together and blend in a spice mill.
- Leave to cool completely and store in airtight bottles or sealed plastic bags.

glossaryofingredients

NYONYA SPECIALTIES – THE BEST OF SINGAPORE'S RECIPES

SPICES ● ● ● ● ○ ○

1. Aniseed
Similar in flavour as star anise, aniseed is popular in Chinese cooking, adding a delicate licorice taste to sweet and savoury dishes. It is available whole, as tiny egg-shaped seeds, or in powdered form and can be bought in health food stores, Chinese delicatessens and some large supermarkets. It is also used in baking, especially biscuits and cakes, in preserving, such as plums and gherkins, in anise-flavoured liqueurs and drinks, and to mask the strong flavours of some cough medicines.

2. Cardamom
Cardamom is the world's most expensive spice after saffron. Cardamom pods are the dried fruits of a perennial plant of the ginger family indigenous to Sri Lanka and south India. The pale green oval pods, which are the best variety, contain 15–20 brown or black seeds. The white pods are simply green pods that have been bleached in the sun.

3, 4, 5. Chilli
Native to Mexico, chillies are now available in many forms – fresh, dried, powdered, flaked as well in the form of sauces, sambal and pastes. They range from mild to wild, and the smaller the chilli, the hotter it is, e.g. bird's eye chillies.

Chillies are used either unripe, when they are green, or ripe, after they turn red. Ripe chillies are hotter then green ones. Red chillies are usually pounded or ground into a paste, chopped or used whole for flavouring, or cut in different ways for garnishing. Green chillies are generally used whole for flavouring, or cut in different ways, for garnishing. Both red and green chillies are also available pickled. Dried chillies are pounded or ground and used for flavouring and seasoning.

Related to cayenne and Tabasco chillies, the colour of bird's eye chillies may range from deep red to cream, yellow or orange. Thin-fleshed with a deep fiery heat, its flavour may range from mild to sweet.

6. Cinnamon
Cinnamon, the edible bark of the tree native to Sri Lanka, is probably the most popular cooking spice in the Western world. The innermost layer of the bark is sold as thin, fragile quills in India, Sri Lanka, Indonesia and Malaysia and Singapore and is used for flavouring meat, poultry and desserts. The spice is also available powdered, but its flavour and aroma dissipate rather quickly in this form.

7. Clove
Cloves are actually the flower buds of a tree of the myrtle family indigenous to the Maluku Island (Moluccas) or the Spice Islands. The buds are harvested and dried under the sun for days. Cloves have a stronger flavour than most other spices and are therefore used in smaller quantities.

8. Coriander seeds
With their clean, lemony flavour, coriander seeds are a major component of most curry powder used in India, Sri Lanka, Indonesia, Malaysia and other countries. Freshly ground coriander is more fragrant than coriander that is purchased already powdered.

9. Cumin
Cumin is used in Middle Eastern, Asian and Mediterranean cooking. This aromatic spice has a nutty flavour and is available whole or ground. It is popularly used to flavour curries, stews and Indian yoghurt drinks (lassi).

10. Fenugreek
The seeds and tender sprouted leaves of fenugreek, native to Europe and Asia, are both edible. The seeds, with their bitter flavour, are an important component of Indian curry powders. The seeds are also used whole in some Sri Lankan and Malaysian dishes, particularly seafood curries.

11. Five-spice powder
Frequently used in all sorts of Chinese dishes, it summons up the taste and smell of China. As the name implies, it is made up of five ground spices – Szechuan pepper, cinnamon, clove, fennel seeds and star anise.

Available from delicatessens, Chinese markets and some health food shops, it should be kept in a sealed container in a dry place. Like most spices, it will keep for several months but will gradually lose its fragrance and flavour and therefore should not be kept for too long.

12. Galangal
Greater galangal is native to Malaysia and Java. It has a delicate flavour and is used fresh in Malaysian, Indonesian and Thai cooking. When the fresh variety is not available, dried and powdered galangal can be used instead.

The young rhizome is pale pink and is more tender and flavourful than the mature one, which is beige in colour. Galangal belongs to the ginger family but cannot be used as a substitute for the common ginger, as its pungency and tang is distinctively different. It is added to curries or dishes in slices, chunks or as a paste. As it is quite fibrous, chop it into small pieces before pounding or grinding it.

13. Garlic
Garlic is used with almost anything, except maybe dessert. Its flavour depends on how it is prepared – cooked garlic being much milder than raw, chopped garlic. It can be used raw or fried, poached, roasted or sautéed, and can be cooked peeled or unpeeled. Choose a firm, hard head of garlic with no soft or discoloured patches. Do not refrigerate but store in a cool, dry place.

14. Ginger
Ginger, a fleshy rhizome, is used in the West to make gingerbread, ginger beer, candied ginger and chocolate ginger. Fresh ginger is a basic ingredient in many Asian cuisines. It is usually sliced, finely chopped, pounded or ground and used in savoury dishes. Sometimes the juice is extracted and used.

15. Nutmeg
Buy whole and grate as needed. Nutmeg is used to flavour soups, vegetables, breads and cakes. A true Bolognese sauce is not complete without grated nutmeg.

16. Onion
Onions are indispensable in our day-to-day cooking. There are dry onions and green onions. Dry onions are left in the ground to mature and have a tougher, outer skin for longer storage. Green onions are merely young and immature. There are many varieties and many ways to use them.

17. Oom (ajowan) seeds
Also called omum seed, carom seed or Bishop's weed, this is the small seed of a herb belonging to the cumin and parsley family, and has the flavour of thyme. It is used sparingly in Indian lentil dishes and pickles due to its strong flavour.

18, 19. Pepper
Peppers are small, round berries that grow in trailing clusters. They start off a deep green and turn red as they ripen. Black pepper is obtained by drying the green berries in the sun, which makes the outer skin black and shrivelled.

White pepper is obtained by packing the ripe berries in sacks, soaking them in slow-flowing water for eight days and then rubbing off the softened outer skin. The inner portion is then dried in the sun for several days until it turns a creamy white. White pepper is hotter than black pepper, but it is not as fragrant.

20. Shallot
A small bulb with a sweeter, lighter, more delicate flavour than an onion. There are a number of varieties including grey, pink and brown. Most easily obtained in spring and summer, shallots are often required in dishes from France.

21. Star anise
Star anise comes from a tree belonging to the magnolia family. The dried eight-pointed star-shaped pod is used for flavouring meat and poultry dishes in Malaysia, Singapore, Indonesia, China and Vietnam.

22. Turmeric
This yellow coloured rhizome is related to ginger and used in many dishes in India. It is also added to Thai curries. The fresh root has an aromatic and spicy fragrance, which can be lost by drying. Turmeric is available fresh or powdered. In a recipe, 1 Tbsp chopped turmeric is equivalent to $1/4$ tsp powdered turmeric.

VEGETABLES

23. Bamboo shoots
These are the young shoots of the bamboo. Fresh bamboo shoots must be boiled for at least 1 hour to soften before they can be used. After boiling, soak them in water until required. Boiled and ready-to-use bamboo shoots are available in packets or canned from Chinese grocery stores and some supermarkets.

24. Bean sprouts
In Asia, bean sprouts are grown from either mung beans (green beans) or soy beans, while in the west they are always grown from mung beans. If the sprouts are intended to be eaten raw, they should be mung bean sprouts. Soy bean sprouts have to be cooked for 10 minutes before they can be eaten.

25. Bilimbi
This small fruit, locally known as *belimbing asam* or *belimbing buluh*, is light green or yellow in colour and resembles a tiny cucumber. It has a sour taste. Fresh bilimbi is added to dishes such as *sambal* and curries to tenderise the meat and to give a tangy flavour. This versatile fruit can be pickled or preserved with salt and then dried and used as a substitute for tamarind (*asam*).

26. Bittergourd
This wrinkled, cucumber-like vegetable is eaten while still unripe. With bitter tasting flesh which improves when cooked, the bittergourd features in Southeast Asian dishes such as cooked salads and stir-fries. It is also made into a tart pickle and is popular in India. According to Asian kitchen wisdom, the more grooves on the bittergourd, the more bitter it will be.

27. Brinjal
This vegetable comes in two varieties – egg-shape and long. They are either white or deep purple. The purple variety has a thicker skin, but there is no difference in flavour.

28. Cabbage
Cabbage is related to broccoli, cauliflower, kohlrabi and Brussels sprouts. Choose heads which are heavy with crisp, shiny outer leaves. Eat raw in salads. Cook only for a minimum time in a covered saucepan and drain very well.

29. Carrot
Choose bright orange, shiny specimens; avoid those with soft spots or cracks or those, which are limp. In spring, look for baby carrots with their green tops intact. Serve cooked or raw in salads.

30. Chinese mustard, preserved
This is the most commonly used preserved vegetable in Chinese cooking. This is Chinese mustard or leaf mustard that has been preserved in vinegar (*kiam chye*) and can keep indefinitely. It is used in stir fries and soups.

31. Cucumber
Although cucumbers are usually thought of as essential for salads and with crudités, it is also surprisingly good when braised and served as a vegetable, especially with fish and seafood dishes. Look for glossy, crisp, bright green vegetables.

32. Flowering cabbage
Flowering cabbage (*choy sum*) has green leaves, pale green stems and small yellow flowers. This vegetable can be steamed, stir-fried or blanched and used in noodle dishes, soup, etc.

33. French beans
This name encompasses a range of green beans, including the snap bean and the bobby bean. They are mostly fat and fleshy and when fresh, should be firm so that they break in half with a satisfying snapping sound.

34. Jackfruit
The jackfruit tree, native to India's Western Ghats, bears the world's largest fruit. The fruit is eaten both young and ripe. Green, with thick, sharp pines, the starchy young jackfruit is usually cooked as a vegetable. It is a staple source of starch in many Asian and South Pacific countries, where it is fried, roasted or boiled. When ripe, it is eaten as a fruit or used in some Asian desserts.

35. Jicama
Originating from America, jicama (*bangkuang* or yam bean), locally referred to as 'Chinese turnip', are now cultivated in most countries in Asia. It has one root and is sweet, juicy and crunchy. It is an important ingredient in spring rolls or *poh pia*.

36. Lady's finger
Also called okra, this vegetable belongs to the hibiscus family. It is particularly popular in Creole and Cajun cooking. It has a glutinous texture and is a natural thickener. Soaking for 30 minutes in vinegar, diluted with water, can minimize the viscosity.

37. Long beans
Also known as the Chinese bean, this very long, narrow, dark green variety is cooked as you would a green bean.

38. Papaya

Indigenous to Central America, papayas range in size from very small to very large, and are eaten both ripe and green. When ripe, the papaya has soft juicy flesh and a fairly sweet taste (similar to apricot); it makes a good dessert or breakfast fruit. The unripe fruit, which has crisp, firm, tangy flesh, can be cooked as a vegetable, made into salads or used to make preserves and pickles. The fruit is very popular in Asia, where the flowers, leaves and young stem of the papaya tree are also cooked and eaten.

39. Pineapple

Native to South America, the pineapple is really a cluster of fruits of the Ananas tree that combine to form one 'multiple fruit'. The pineapple is one of the most popular tropical fruits. Available all year round, it makes an excellent dessert fruit. It can be bought fresh or canned. The fruit is delicious eaten ripe. In Asia, semi-ripe pineapple is used in sour soups and curries.

40. Pisang raja

These uniformly-shaped bananas are long and slim. When ripe, the skin is pale yellow and has a sweet fragrance. These bananas are popularly used in *goreng pisang*, where they are coated in batter and deep-fried as a tasty snack.

41. Potato

Originates from South America, potatoes are an important source of carbohydrates. Once thought to be fattening, potatoes can be part of a calorie-controlled diet. They are low in sodium, high in potassium and an important source of complex carbohydrates and vitamins C and B-6, as well as a storehouse of minerals.

Potatoes are available year-round. Choose potatoes that are suitable for the desired method of cooking. All potatoes should be firm, well-shaped (for their type) and blemish-free. New potatoes may be missing some of their feathery skin but other types should not have any bald

spots. Avoid potatoes that are wrinkled, sprouted or cracked. Store potatoes in a cool, dark, well-ventilated place for up to 2 weeks. Warm temperatures encourage sprouting and shriveling.

42. Sugarcane

This is a tall Southeast Asian grass which has stout, fibrous, jointed stalks. These juicy canes produce sap which is a source of molasses and commercial sugar. In this part of the world, sugarcane is often squeezed to extract its juice and is drunk ice cold; cut into short lengths and chewed for its juice or boiled with water chestnuts to make a traditional Chinese tea.

43. Sweet potato

This elongated tuber comes in orange, white, yellow and purple. It is commonly used to make Asian desserts and is also added to salads to replace the potato. Prepare and cook as you would potatoes.

44. Tapioca

Tapioca in its fresh form is called yucca, which is another name for the root of the cassava plant. This root is also known as manioc or mandioca. When raw, it has a bland and sticky quality and is used in cooking the way you would a potato. It can be boiled, mashed or fried.

45. Tomato

Native to South America, dozens of tomato varieties are available today — ranging widely in size, shape and colour. Among the most commonly marketed are the beefsteak tomato, globe tomato, plum tomato and the small cherry tomato.

Choose firm, well-shaped tomatoes that are noticeably fragrant and richly coloured. They should be free from blemishes, heavy for their size and give slightly to palm pressure. Ripe tomatoes should be stored at room temperature and used within a few days. They should never be refrigerated — cold temperatures make the flesh pulpy and kills the flavour.

Unripe fruit can be ripened by placing it in a pierced paper bag with an apple for several days at room temperature but do not refrigerate or set in the sun.

Tomatoes are rich in vitamin C and contain amounts of vitamins A and B, potassium, iron and phosphorus.

46. Water convolvulus

A green leafy vegetable, water convolvulus (*kangkung*) can be found growing wild beside streams. Some varieties have purple stems. If unavailable, substitute with spinach or watercress.

47. White radish

Also called daikon or mooli, it looks rather like a large white carrot, hence its Chinese name which literally means 'white carrot'. With a mild flavour and an ability to soak up other flavours, it is excellent for braising or used in delicate Chinese soups. It is also pickled.

HERBS

48. Basil leaf

Asian basil, also known as sweet basil, is widely used in Thailand. Several varieties are used to flavour foods. The sweet, aromatic fragrance of *bai horapa* graces many dishes while *maenglak*, or lemon basil, is used in soups. Basil leaves are best used fresh as they do not retain their flavour when dried.

49. Chinese celery

Similar in appearance to continental parsley, this is a stronger flavoured version of the more familiar celery. The colour may vary from white to dark green. Use in soups, stir-fries and stews.

50. Chinese chives

Also known as garlic chives, Chinese chives have thick, long flat leaves like the spring onion (scallion) and a stronger flavour than the Western chives. It is used both as a herb and vegetable in Southeast Asian cooking.

51. Chinese parsley

Also known as coriander leaves or cilantro, Chinese parsley is indigenous to southern Europe. All parts of the plant can be used, even the roots, which are an essential ingredient in Thai cooking. This herb is used to flavour and garnish dishes.

52. Curry leaves

Sprigs of small, shiny pointed leaves with a distinctive fragrance, curry leaves are used most frequently in south India , Sri Lanka, Malaysia and Singapore and Fiji. Fresh curry leaves are normally sautéed with onions while making curry. Dried curry leaves, which are probably easier to find in Western countries, are not as strongly flavoured, but they serve the purpose.

53. Kaffir lime leaves

These are the leaves from the kaffir lime plant. The lime is a small dark green citrus fruit with a thick, wrinkled and bumpy rind. Its leaves are easily recognised by its two distinct sections. The leaves are available fresh or dried, and are used in soups, curries and stir-fries.

54. Lemon grass

Lemon grass, a long lemon-scented grass, is popular for flavouring curries and soups in Malaysia and Singapore , Indonesia, Thailand and other Southeast Asian countries. Only the pale lower portion of the stem, with the tough outer layers peeled away, is used for cooking. If lemon grass is not available, two or three strips of thinly peeled lemon zest can be used as a substitute.

55. Mint leaves

There are over 30 species of mint, the two most popular and widely available being peppermint and spearmint. Peppermint is the more pungent of the two. It has bright green leaves, purple-tinged stems and a peppery flavour. Spearmint leaves are gray-green or true green and have a milder flavour and fragrance. Mint grows wild throughout the world and is cultivated in Europe, the United States and Asia. It's most plentiful during summer months but many markets carry it year-round.

Choose leaves that are evenly coloured with no sign of wilting. Store a bunch of mint, stems down, in a glass of water with a plastic bag over the leaves. Refrigerate in this manner for up to a week, changing the water every 2 days. Mint is available fresh, dried, as an extract and in the form of oil of spearmint or oil of peppermint, both highly concentrated flavourings.

56. Polygonum leaves

These narrow, pointed leaves are also known as Vietnamese mint and *laksa* leaves. They are used for garnishing and flavouring curries. The leaves are either crushed or sliced and used in curries or *laksa*. The leaves are also added to fish dishes to camouflage the fishy smell.

57. Screwpine leaves

Commonly known as *pandan* leaf, the long narrow leaf is used in Singapore, Malaysia, Indonesia and Thailand in savoury dishes and desserts. The leaves, with their delicate flavour, are as essential to Asian cooking as the vanilla essence is to Western cooking. When pounded and strained to extract the juice, the leaves lend flavour and colour to Asian sweets and desserts. They can also be used to wrap marinated meat and other food to add flavour.

58. Spring onions

Spring onions, known as scallions in the United States, have long thin leaves with sometimes a white bulb at the base. Both the white and green portions are chopped and used for garnishing.

59. Torch ginger flower

This bud of the wild ginger flower has a delicate aroma. For cooking purposes, the bud is picked while the petals are still tightly folded. Its intriguing fragrance lends a refreshing aroma to curries and fish dishes. The bud may be eaten raw, where it is finely sliced and added to vegetable salads such as *kerabu* or *rojak*. The full blossom is added to soups and gravies to impart its unique flavour.

60. Turmeric leaf

The leaves of the turmeric plant are very fragrant and used extensively in curries. It is usually shredded to impart a stronger flavour.

FLAVOURING

61, 62. Coconut (whole & grated)

Coconut is indispensable in Malaysian, Singaporean, Indonesian and Thai kitchens. Coconut milk is not the water found in the middle of the coconut; rather it is the liquid extracted from the grated flesh of the coconut. The first extraction is the richest and is called the No.1 milk. Water is then added to the already used coconut flesh and squeezed again to extract a slightly weaker milk referred to as the No.2 milk.

Roasted grated coconut is often added to enrich certain dishes. This is obtained by roasting fresh grated coconut, stirring constantly in a dry pan over low heat until it turns golden brown.

Coconut milk and grated coconut can be found in supermarkets, fresh, canned or powdered, which can then be reconstituted with the addition of water.

63. Kaffir lime

(*See 51. Kaffir lime leaves.*)

64. Kalamansi lime

The juice of this small, round, green citrus fruit is very sour. It adds a tangy flavour to dishes and drinks. It is also referred to as 'local lime'.

65. Lime

This small, lemon-shaped citrus fruit has a thin green skin and a juicy, pale green pulp. Limes grow in tropical and subtropical climes such as Mexico, California, Florida and the Caribbean.

Look for brightly coloured, smooth-skinned limes that are heavy for their size. Small brown areas on the skin won't affect flavour or succulence but a hard or shriveled skin will. Refrigerate uncut limes in a plastic bag for up to 10 days. Cut limes can be stored in the same way up to 5 days. The versatile lime has a multitude of uses, from a sprightly addition to mixed drinks to a marinade for raw fish dishes to the famous desserts.

52

53

54

55

56

57

58

59

60

61

62

63

64

65

OTHER INGREDIENTS ● ● ● ● ○

66. Almond
Almond is the kernel of the fruit of the almond tree, grown extensively in California, the Mediterranean, Australia and South Africa. There are two main types — sweet and bitter. The flavour of sweet almonds is delicate and slightly sweet. They are readily available in markets and, unless otherwise indicated, are the variety used in recipes. The more strongly flavoured bitter almonds contain traces of lethal prussic acid when raw.

Almonds are available blanched or not, whole, sliced, chopped, candied, smoked, in paste form and in many flavours. Toasting almonds before using in recipes intensifies their flavour and adds crunch.

67. Anchovy, dried
These are salted and sun-dried anchovies. They are available in wet markets and Chinese grocery stores. To store them, remove the head and intestines, rinse quickly and dry thoroughly before storing. Fry them in deep fat when they are dry and they make delicious, crisp snacks that go well with drinks.

68. Black prawn paste
This prawn paste is not to be confused with the dried shrimp paste, or *belacan,* which is more commonly used in Asian cooking. Neither can this be used as a substitute for *belacan.* Black prawn paste (*kay ko* or *petis*) is a black, molasses-like paste made from shrimp, sugar, salt, flour and water. It is most famously used in Penang *laksa*. It is often an acquired

taste and has a smoky, earthy pungent flavour.

69. Candlenut
This hard, waxy and beige nut has a slightly bitter taste. Small quantities are pounded or blended into a paste and used as a natural thickener. It also adds a nutty texture and flavour to curry dishes. To prevent it from becoming rancid, store candlenuts in an airtight container in the refrigerator.

70. Char siew
This is lean roasted pork where the surface of the roast has been coloured red. It is often sold alongside roast duck.

71. Chicken stock cube
Chicken stock is obtained by boiling and simmering of chicken bones and carcass for several hours. The stock is strained and refrigerated then its solidified fat that rises on the surface is removed to get a virtually fat-free stock. This stock is then freezed in ice cube trays for future use. Chicken stock is used to give flavours to the dishes.

Ready-made chicken stock cubes can be bought at the supermarkets.

72. Chinese cruellers
These are long fritters of dough which has been deep fried in pairs, so they stick together. In Taiwan, it is eaten for breakfast with soy bean milk. In Singapore and Malaysia, it is often chopped and added to porridge or to *tau suan*, a hot dessert made of green beans. Its name is literally translated to 'oil fried devils', and refers to the fate of a husband-and-wife pair in ancient China who

betrayed a well-loved hero.

73. Chinese mushrooms, dried
This is dried shiitake mushrooms and varies in size and price, depending on quality. Soak them in hot water before use. Add the soaking liquid to add to the dish while cooking, or into stocks to lend a richer flavour.

74. Cloud ear fungus
This white fungus should be soaked in water to soften before use. When soaked, it bloats into a large, crunchy sheet. With no taste of its own, it offers a crunchy texture and is commonly used in Chinese stir-fries or desserts.

75. Crisp-fried shallots
Crisp-fried shallots are shallots that have been sliced fine and deep-fried in hot cooking oil until golden brown. They are used for flavouring and garnishing. To make them at home, peel the shallots and finely slice them crosswise. Deep-fry in hot oil over low heat, stirring briskly all the while. Turn off the heat as soon as they turn a pale brown. Remove and drain on absorbent paper until cool. Store in an airtight container.

76. Dried prawns
These are sun-dried, salted, steamed prawns. Soak them in water for about 20 minutes to remove excess salt before using. Dried prawns are ground, chopped or left whole and fried to flavour dishes.

77. Dried sour fruit slices
Dried sour fruit (*asam gelugur*) slices is a tangerine-like fruit that is

sliced thinly and dried in the sun. Light brown when fresh, it turns darker as it ages. Like tamarind (*asam*), it is used to give acidity to cooked food.

Dried sour fruit slices are usually available from Chinese grocery stores. If not available, substitute with tamarind pulp.

78. Fish maw
Fish maw is the air bladder of the fish. Its main function is to receive and expel huge qualities of water and/or oxygen so that fish can ascend and descend in the water. This makes the bladder very strong and elastic. Dried fish maw is mostly used in the preparation of thick soup. It is effective in relieving coughs and beneficial for the general health.

79. Golden needles
These are unopened flower buds of orange and yellow day lillies. At certain times of year, you may find fresh lily buds in Asian produce markets, with bright golden petals tightly folded above an emerald green calyx. They are delicious stir-fried with minced pork and flavoured with garlic, black pepper and fish sauce. Lily buds are known as 'golden needles' because of their original colour, though once dried, they fade to a pale brown. Popular with Buddhists and other vegetarians, they add a distinctive, earthy flavour to a dish.

The long, slender dried buds of the day lily (*kim chiam*) are sold in packets and will keep well if stored airtight. Look for buds pale in colour and still flexible, not

dark brown and brittle, which indicates they are old. Store in a jar with a tight-fitting lid, away from the light. Before adding to a dish, soak in warm water for 20–30 minutes. Trim soaked buds of hard stem, then either tie each in a knot, shred by tearing, or cut across in halves.

80. Indonesian black nut
Although native to Brazil, this black, hard-shelled nut known locally as *buah keluak,* is grown extensively in Indonesia. The black oily kernel has a slightly bitter taste. A good nut is heavy, does not rattle when shaken and does not produce a hollow sound when tapped lightly.

81. Lime paste
A white substance obtained by burning and grinding cockle shells until fine. It is usually eaten with betel leaves. It is available in some speciality baking stores.

82. Orange peel, dried
Often added to soups and casseroles, it gives a distinct and pleasant orange flavour. The best peel comes from large, brightly coloured fruit. The peel is threaded into twine and dried in the sun for a week. It is often sold in packets and can be bought from most Chinese grocery stores or herbalists. Soak for 20 minutes before use. Keeps indefinitely if stored in an airtight container.

83. Palm sugar
Also known as jaggery, palm sugar is made from the sap of the palm tree. Fresh palm sap is boiled into a concento solidify into cylindrical shapes. Palm sugar, also

66

67

68

69

70

71

72

73

74

75

76

77

78

79

80

81

82

known as *gula Melaka* or *gula kabung* in Malaysia and *gula Jawa* or *aren* in Indonesia, is used for both savoury dishes and sweets.

84. Peanuts
The nuts have a papery brown skin and are contained in a thin, netted, tan-coloured pod. Peanuts are also called groundnuts or earth nuts because, after flowering, the plant bends down to the earth and buries its pods in the ground. Peanuts are sold unshelled and shelled. The former should have clean, unbroken shells and should not rattle when shaken. Shelled peanuts, often available in vacuum-sealed jars or cans, are usually roasted and sometimes salted. Refrigerate unshelled peanuts tightly wrapped for up to 6 months.

85. *Poh pia* skin
These are large, tissue-thin skins of rice flour dough which are used for making spring rolls. They are sold in packets of 25 or 50, and if frozen, should be thoroughly thawed before using. They are becoming widely available in supermarkets,

though some specialty artisans still make them fresh and continue to be in great demand among *poh pia* aficionados. Keep unused wrappers in plastic wrap or covered with a damp cloth until ready to use; once they have dried out, they break easily and become impossible to fold.

86. Preserved Tientsin cabbage
This brownish-green pieces of the stem of the Chinese cabbage that has been preserved in brine (*tung chye*). It has a savoury, mildly salty flavour and a firm, crisp texture. Sold in jars, it can be bought from Oriental markets. Rinse thoroughly before use.

87. Processed cuttlefish
The cuttlefish, which resembles a rather large squid, has 10 appendages and can reach up to 6.5 metres in length. It can be prepared like its less tender relatives, the squid and octopus, but must still be tenderized before cooking in order not to be exceedingly chewy. Cuttlefish are most popular in Japan, India and many Mediterranean

countries. Dried cuttlefish is available in some Asian markets. It should be reconstituted before cooking. To reconstitute, soak in warm water for several hours, then simmer in clean water.

88. Red beans
Also known as adzuki or aduki beans, red beans are usually cooked during celebrations in China and Japan because red is considered an auspicious and lucky colour. The beans are usually boiled with sugar and mashed to make fillings for sweet cakes or sweet soups.

89. Salted fish, Penang
Dried and salted fish are a Malaysian speciality. Highly flavourful, it is used in small amounts in curries and sambals. It is also added to stir fries to lift an otherwise bland dish.

90. Salted radish
This is finely diced radish preserved in spices and salt to get golden-brown morsels that are crisp and eaten as a relish (*chai poh*). There is also another type known in Chinese as *tai tou choy*. The latter is made from whole radish cut into slices

lengthwise and with all the leaves intact, salted and dried.

91. Sesame seeds
Native to India, sesame seeds have a strong, pleasant, nutty flavour and are frequently used in breads, salads and to make oil. They are available in black and white varieties.

92. Shrimp paste
Dried shrimp paste is made from small shrimps, which have been dried in the sun before being pounded into a paste. This strong smelling condiment is widely used in Malay and Nyonya cooking. It is pounded and blended with other spices and seasonings to make a spice mix which is the base for *sambal* dishes, curries and spicy gravies. Dried shrimp paste can be bought fresh whole or as pre-roasted granules.

93. Sugared winter melon
This is winter melon crystallised in sugar (*tung kwa*). Often sold in the dried foods section of a Chinese grocery or supermarket, it is used in various Chinese desserts (*tong sui*) and home made barley water.

94. Tamarind pulp
The tamarind fruit or *asam*, is commonly used in Southeast Asian cooking. The long pods contain pulp-covered seeds, which are usually dried and sold. This pulp is soaked in water for about 10 minutes and strained of any fibres and seeds. The sour juice is used, and adds fragrance and flavour to dishes.

95. Wheat
Wheat is the world's largest cereal-grass crop. Its status as a staple is second only to rice. Wheat contains a relatively high amount of gluten, the protein that provides the elasticity necessary for excellent breadmaking. Though there are over 30,000 varieties, the three major types are hard wheat, soft wheat and durum wheat.

96. Yellow bean paste
Popular in Nyonya cooking, this light brown paste is made of preserved soy beans, and lends an earthy, salty flavour to dishes. A variation of this paste incorporates chilli and is sold as spicy bean paste.

83

84

85

86

87

88

89

90

91

92

93

94

95

96

SOY BEAN PRODUCTS

NOODLES ● ● ● ● ●

WRAPPER

97. Bean curd (firm and soft)

Firm bean curd (*taukwa*) is pressed and quite heavy. It is the firmest bean curd of all and very versatile.

Soft bean curd is available in slabs from the wet market or in rectangular containers and tubes from the supermarket. It has the texture of custard. Handle carefully to prevent breaking it. There are several varieties of bean curd including silken bean curd and cotton bean curd which is slightly firmer, but not as firm as *taukwa*. It is also available combined with egg, and sold as 'egg bean curd'. These are often cylindrical in shape and sport a distinctive yellow shade.

98. Bean curd puffs

Known as *taupok*, these are deep-fried bean curd puffs, which are either round or square in shape. They are light, with a golden brown exterior and a soft, somewhat 'honeycomb' interior. Whether it is stuffed with fish or meat, or is eaten as it is, it has an easy to chew texture, which gives it a very distinctive taste. Like all bean curd, it absorbs other flavours well.

99, 100. Bean curd skin and sticks

Dried bean curd skin can be found in stick and strips (*foo chok*) or sheets (*foo pei*). This comes from the thin, yellow layer that forms on the surface of soy bean milk before it coagulates. *Foo chok* is commonly used in desserts. *Foo pei* comes in sheets about 60-cm wide. They are sold folded like plastic sheets and are available at stores selling bean curd, Chinese grocery stores and supermarkets. Do not refrigerate them.

101. Sweet bean curd strips (*tim chok*)

These are small, seasoned, brown rectangular pieces of dried bean curd known as *tim chok*. These are used mainly in vegetarian cooking.

102. Cellophane noodles

The vermicelli-like noodles are made from mung bean flour. They are also called glass noodles or bean starch noodles. They should be soaked in water before being added to boiling soups or stir-fried vegetables. Cellophane noodles are used in Japanese, Thai Burmese, Vietnamese, Chinese, Malaysian, Philippine and Indonesian cooking.

103. Coarse rice vermicelli, fresh

Made from rice flour, these *laksa* noodles are as thick as spaghetti. Dried rice vermicelli can be used as a substitute if fresh noodles are not available.

104. Fine wheat vermicelli

These Filipino off-white dried wheat noodles (*mee suah*) are very slender. They can be deep-fried to make a crunchy nest or boiled for 2–3 minutes to make a salad or be added directly to soup.

105. Rice noodles

Made from rice flour, these flat, opaque noodles (*kway teow*) are about 1-cm (¹/₂-in) wide. They are available fresh or dried and can be boiled or fried. Dried noodles should be soaked for up to 30 minutes to soften.

106. Rice vermicelli

Rice vermicelli (*bee hoon*) is made from rice flour. It can be fried or cooked in a soup. The dried variety needs to be soaked first in cold or hot water to soften, then drained, before cooking.

107. Yellow egg noodles

These large, yellow noodles are made of wheat and are either round (often called Hokkien noodles) or slightly flattened (*mee pok*). They should be rinsed and drained thoroughly before being fried. Like all fresh noodles, they should not be kept for more than a day before using, otherwise they tend to become heavy.

108. Banana leaf

Used in almost every Asian country, the banana leaf is often shaped into cones, square containers, neat rectangular packages to be used as wrappers, or to take the place of a plate. When used as a plate, the mid-rib of the leaf is retained. As a wrapper, the mid-rib is removed. Before shaping it, blanch the banana leaf in boiling water briefly to render it pliable.

97

98

99

100

101

102

103

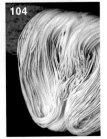

104

105

106

107

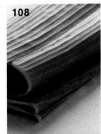

108

INDEX TO THE GLOSSARY OF INGREDIENTS